Mundaka

UPANISHAD

Essence and Sanskrit Grammar

Ashwini Kumar Aggarwal

जय गुरुदेव

© 2020, Ashwini Kumar Aggarwal

ISBN13: 978-81-944890-3-0 Paperback Edition
ISBN13: 978-81-944890-4-7 Hardbound Edition
ISBN13: 978-81-944890-5-4 Digital Edition

This work is licensed under a Creative Commons Attribution 4.0 International License. Please visit https://creativecommons.org/licenses/by/4.0/

Title: Mundaka Upanishad
SubTitle: Essence and Sanskrit Grammar

Printed and Published by
Devotees of Sri Sri Ravi Shankar Ashram
34 Sunny Enclave, Devigarh Road
Patiala 147001, Punjab, India

https://advaita56.weebly.com/
The Art of Living Centre

https://www.artofliving.org/

10th January2020, Pausha Poornima, Arudra Darshan
Ardra Nakshatra, Hemant Ritu, World Hindi Divas
Vikram Samvat 2076 Paridhavi, Saka Era 1941 Vikari

1st Edition January 2020

जय गुरुदेव

Dedication

Sri Sri Ravi Shankar

who impressed upon us —
the Intellect is nurtured and made RAZOR sharp by
Spirituality

Preface

Questions are many, answers galore. **Paths are many, the goal is One.**

Only the brave seeks beyond the obvious. Only the enduring is no longer fascinated by the sensuous.

He then knocks at the door. He turns towards Spirituality. He shuns distractions. His steps lead him to the Master. He sits in awe at the Master's feet. Upanishad happens.

Veda	
Mantra Verses (Samhita)	Brahmana Verses
	Brahmana Aranyaka Upanishad

Adi Shankaracharya's masterly commentary on eleven Upanishads is the de facto standard for Vedanta. These eleven have been named the principal Upanishads. Though it is said there are 1180 Upanishads written over a period of a thousand years, actual manuscripts available as of now are 108 only.

A chart that lists the eleven Upanishads commented on in detail by Sankara.

Rigveda	Samaveda	<u>Shukla Yajurveda</u> Krishna Yajurveda	Atharvaveda
Gives the fundamental laws of creation	Gives the intrinsic harmony within creation	Gives the specific design, administrative and governing principles for a family or a nation	Gives the specific ritucharya and dinacharya for an individual
Aitareya	Kena **Chandogya**	Ishavasya **<u>Brihadaranyaka</u>** Katha Taittiriya Shvetashvatara	**Mandukya** Mundaka Prashna
प्रज्ञानम् ब्रह्म	तत् त्वम् असि	अहं ब्रह्म अस्मि	अयम् आत्मा ब्रह्म

Four great illuminating statements or mahavakyas are listed above with their corresponding Upanishads in **bold**. The Mundaka has its very own mahavakya - कस्मिन् विज्ञाते सर्वम् इदं विज्ञातं भवति । 1.1.3

Remember that Vedic Sanskrit text cannot be literally translated into English. Thoughts form and words sprout in deep meditation when guided by a living master.

Mundaka Upanishad is from the Gopatha-Brahmana of the Atharva Veda. Whereas its Samhita portion survives in two recensions, after sages Paippalada and Shaunaka, the Brahmana portion available today is only of sage Gopatha. The Mandukya verses precede the Mundaka verses, which precede the Prashna verses in the Atharvaveda.

Mundaka Upanishad मुण्डक उपनिषद् gets its name from "a head shaved of all heavy botherations", "an intellect clear of all doubts". By the sincere study of this Upanishad, one's mind resolves all troubles, difficulties seem trifles. It quenches the thirst of the sincere seeker and in beautiful verse satiates the heart of the ardent aspirant.

Mundaka is especially written for the man who is willing to rise above the crowd, whose performance in daily life is extraordinary, who is willing to work harder than his colleagues. It is for the soul who uses his talents to be creative and productive, and is at the same time thirsting for the Unknown.

Table of Contents

PREFACE 4

BLESSING 8

PRAYER 9

1ST YEAR 1ST SEMESTER 10

    The Mysterious Karmic Plane 11

1ST YEAR 2ND SEMESTER 30

    The Laws of Motion 31

2ND YEAR 1ST SEMESTER 56

2ND YEAR 2ND SEMESTER 76

    2.2.4 The chant of Om 83

3RD YEAR 1ST SEMESTER 98

    Story Time... 98
    3.1.1 Nara and Narayana 99

THE FINAL TERM 118

    Freedom 119

ETYMOLOGY OF UPANISHAD 142

LATIN TRANSLITERATION CHART 143

VERSES FOR CHANTING WITH SVARAS 144

SANSKRIT GRAMMAR 150

CONJUGATION PROCESS OF VERB 153

DECLENSION PROCESS OF NOUN 154

REFERENCES 155

EPILOGUE 156

Blessing

"There isn't any botheration that you cannot resolve without the presence of a Master and the *thirst* of a Seeker. Truth unveils only when there is a *capable* Master and an aspiring student."

Sri Sri Ravi Shankar
Vishalakshi Mantap, Bangalore Ashram
15-17 Aug 2015, Bhagavad Gita Chap 8 Hindi Discourse

Acknowledgements

A supremely satisfying Guru Puja Havan at KJ's place followed by a sumptuous Delhi World Book Fair at Pragati Maidan.
10th Jan 2020, Vasant Kunj, New Delhi.

Cover Photo Credits

https://www.pexels.com/photo/red-and-white-tower-under-a-starry-sky-3511571/
Photo by Jan Kopřiva from Pexels.

Prayer

शान्तिपाठः

ॐ भद्रं कर्णेभिः श्रृणुयाम देवाः । भद्रं पश्ये माक्षभिर् यजत्राः ।
स्थिरैरङ्गैस् तुष्टुवाꣲ सस्तनूभिः । व्यशेम देवहितं यदायुः ।
स्वस्ति न इन्द्रो वृद्धश्रवाः । स्वस्ति नꣳ पूषा विश्ववेदाः ।
स्वस्ति नस्ताक्ष्यों अरिष्टनेमिः । स्वस्ति नो बृहस्पतिर्दधातु ॥
ॐ शान्तिः शान्तिः शान्तिः ॥

śāntipāṭhaḥ

oṃ bhadraṃ karṇebhiḥ śṛṇuyāma devāḥ | bhadraṃ
paśye mākṣabhir yajatrāḥ | sthirairaṅgais tuṣṭuvāꣲ
sastanūbhiḥ | vyaśema devahitaṃ yadāyuḥ |
svasti na indro vṛddhaśravāḥ | svasti naꣳ pūṣā
viśvavedāḥ | svasti nastārkṣyo ariṣṭanemiḥ | svasti
no bṛhaspatirdadhātu ‖ oṃ śāntiḥ śāntiḥ śāntiḥ ‖

Peace Invocation

O Lord!
May our senses be fully functional. May our joints be
firm and supple. May our reasoning be without
malice. May our desires be for our welfare and for the
welfare of the entire neighborhood.

May our conscience be up and awake.
May we let go of rigidity, obstinacy, false notions.

Peace in our heart, in our body and in our environs.

अथ मुण्डक उपनिषद् (मुण्डकोपनिषद्)

atha Muṇḍaka Upaniṣad

Now begins the Muṇḍaka

Upaniṣad means a deep connection with Divinity. The inward journey begins when one halts to probe. One merges the small mind into the BIG mind. One catches the wavelength of the Master.

Vowel Sandhi – Guna Sandhi – अ + उ → ओ

मुण्डक + उपनिषद् → मुण्डकोपनिषद् ।

1st Year 1st Semester

Mundaka

= head shaved clean

= ego united with the supreme

= reasoning intellect freed of all doubt

= sensory mind freed from erroneous perception

= guilt washed away from the heart

= impressions rubbed out from the citta so that its innocence is restored.

The Mysterious Karmic Plane

The human plane is designed to live a few lifetimes, say 400 years. Of course with replacements of the anatomical body, since that gets worn out by about 75 years. Those who play the game well over the entire period, of 4 centuries, i.e. with lots of cheerfulness and 100% effort, they automatically attain Brahman. Souls that fail to appreciate the body-mind complex and spend time in grumbling, complaining, back-biting, or rather in being the frog in the well, get another 400 year span. This span is however with a handicap, in the sense that the difficulties are formidable. This means that those who are unlucky enough to repeat the cycle shall have more moments of grief.

However the game ends after 800 years, all souls invariably attain Brahman at the end.

Brahman is the plane of abundance, a plane where all souls are fully nourished and satiated. Then by a desire to explore other realms, some souls go to the karmic plane i.e. to our plane of planet Earth. Other souls go to other realms, of that we shall talk about elsewhere.

ॐ ब्रह्मा देवानां प्रथमः सम्बभूव विश्वस्य कर्ता भुवनस्य गोप्ता ।
स ब्रह्मविद्यां सर्वविद्याप्रतिष्ठामथर्वाय ज्येष्ठपुत्राय प्राह ॥ १.१.१

oṃ brahmā devānāṃ prathamaḥ sambabhūva viśvasya
kartā bhuvanasya goptā | sa brahmavidyāṃ sarvavidyā-
pratiṣṭhāmatharvāya jyeṣṭhaputrāya prāha || 1.1.1

पदच्छेदः

ब्रह्मा देवानां प्रथमः सम्बभूव विश्वस्य कर्ता भुवनस्य गोप्ता ।
सः ब्रह्मविद्यां सर्वविद्या-प्रतिष्ठाम् अथर्वाय ज्येष्ठपुत्राय प्राह ॥

अन्वयः

देवानां $^{m6/1}$ प्रथमः $^{m1/1}$ ब्रह्मा $^{m1/1}$, विश्वस्य $^{n6/1}$ भुवनस्य $^{m6/1}$
कर्ता $^{m1/1}$ गोप्ता $^{m1/1}$ सम्बभूव $^{iii/1}$ लिट् । सः $^{m1/1}$ ब्रह्मविद्यां $^{f2/1}$
सर्वविद्या-प्रतिष्ठाम् $^{f2/1}$ ज्येष्ठपुत्राय $^{m4/1}$ अथर्वाय $^{m4/1}$ प्राह $^{iii/1}$ लिट्
॥

1.1.1 A bit of tradition to create a soothing atmosphere for the great teaching to be delivered by means of a dialogue or satsang.

The eldest member of the family is called the Creator or Progenitor and also Protector or Nourisher. Creator since he is the first to build the home and furnish it with all necessities. Progenitor since he is the one who marries first and raises the family. Brahma is the generic term for grandpa.

We can also consider an inventor or entrepreneur or the one who started it as Brahma.

Brahma also means Protector. Obviously grandpa is the one who implemented whatever was needed for safety for his home, family and neighborhood. Grandpa ensured that his folks were well nurtured and his assets were properly cared for.

The Upanishad very intelligently begins with the word "Brahma" . This serves a number of objects. It is the reason why in the social & cultural traditions in every household, and in every institution the Founder is remembered, praised, and invoked. It helps children and youngsters to imbibe discipline and ingrain character and pragmatism.

Brahma is praised as देवाणां प्रथमः the First among the Intelligent beings = homo sapiens. Brahma's birth is termed सम्बभूव = gratefulness for the birth of

Intelligence. In any family, the brightest son or daughter is called सम्बभूव , meaning the one whose birth makes the family (or an institute) exalted.

Now what did Grandpa do? He imparted the sum total of his life's experience = ब्रह्मविद्यां, i.e. the complete knowledge of all subjects he was adept at सर्वविद्याप्रतिष्ठां, to his eldest progeny ज्येष्ठपुत्राय । Notice the placement of a very crucial word अथर्वाय = the one well versed in economic affairs, dutiful, hardworking, skilled, and upholding family name and tradition. In other words. Grandpa or the Founder of a Company, imparts key knowledge and painstakingly trains only the One who aptly qualifies for the position of successor. Continuing from previous verse, the next verse also adds color and atmosphere to the stage ambience by giving some background information.

अथर्वणे यां प्रवदेत ब्रह्माथर्वा तां पुरोवाचाङ्गिरे ब्रह्मविद्याम् ।
स भारद्वाजाय सत्यवहाय प्राह भारद्वाजोऽङ्गिरसे परावराम् ॥ १.१.२
atharvaṇe yāṃ pravadeta brahmātharvā tāṃ purovācāṅgire brahmavidyām | sa bhāradvājāya satyavahāya prāha bhāradvājo'ṅgirase parāvarām || 1.1.2

अथर्वणे यां प्रवदेत ब्रह्मा अथर्वा तां पुरोवाच अङ्गिरे ब्रह्मविद्याम् ।
स भारद्वाजाय सत्यवहाय प्राह भारद्वाजः अङ्गिरसे परावराम् ॥

1.1.2 Now this body of invaluable experiential wisdom first shared by Grandpa Brahma to his worthy successor Atharvan, was in turn added upon and disseminated. The worthy heir of yore propounded it to अङ्गिरः i.e. to the select body of people or parliament or heads of staff.

Once we have a training methodology and the resources and tools for dissemination of our vision and mission, then we call all the officers of the company and brief them. This is how the system operates and it percolates down to the populace.

Then सत्यवहः or the One who shares the whole truth without editing or abstracting, is adept at choosing the proper words, and has a flair for imparting; is selected to head अङ्गिरसः i.e. the University (or Institution or Company or Nation).

Also सत्यवहः has the adjective भारद्वाजः, i.e. endowed with speed, strength, integrity and tirelessness. The word अङ्गिरसः means a collection of Professors or Masters or Sages who can take the vision forward in a very holistic manner परावराम् ।

Guru is then the one to whom a big businessman or a big leader or one who has seen enough of wealth and is seeking liberation, approaches.

शौनको ह वै महाशालोऽङ्गिरसं विधिवदुपसन्नः पप्रच्छ ।
कस्मिन् नु भगवो विज्ञाते सर्वमिदं विज्ञातं भवतीति ॥ १.१.३

śaunako ha vai mahāśālo'ṅgirasaṃ vidhivadupasannaḥ
papraccha | kasmin nu bhagavo vijñāte sarvamidaṃ
vijñātaṃ bhavatīti ‖ 1.1.3

शौनकः ह वै महाशालः अङ्गिरसं विधिवत् उपसन्नः पप्रच्छ ।
कस्मिन् नु भगवः विज्ञाते सर्वम् इदं विज्ञातं भवति इति ॥

शौनकः $^{m1/1}$ ह ^{0} वै ^{0} महाशालः $^{m1/1}$ विधिवत् ^{0} उपसन्नः $^{PPPm1/1}$
अङ्गिरसं $^{m2/1}$ पप्रच्छ $^{iii/1}$ लिट् ।
भगवः $^{Vm1/1}$ नु ^{0} कस्मिन् $^{n7/1}$ विज्ञाते $^{PPPn7/1}$, सर्वम् $^{n1/1}$ इदं $^{n1/1}$
विज्ञातं $^{PPPn1/1}$ भवति $^{iii/1}$ लट् ।
इति ^{0} ॥

1.1.3 Shaunaka i.e. the one satiated with wealth and thence turning to philosophy, goes seeking Angiras - the Guru. On meeting the Guru, he pays due respects first by serving the Guru, attending to his needs, i.e. seeing the Guru is well-fed and well-clothed and well-rested.

Then Shaunaka poses the Mahavakya - the Ultimate Question -

"O Dear Lord! What is it that being known, all this becomes known?".
"O Dear Lord! What is it that being understood, life's puzzle becomes clear?".

The devotee is asking how he may come to terms with life's ups and downs. How may the storms of passion and the vagaries of senses be cheerfully handled. How may the mind be cleansed of doubt and the heart be rid of fear and guilt? What is the way to unite with the Divine? What is the key to Liberation?

or simply

How may he just do what he has set out to do? (more or less on a regular basis!)

तस्मै स होवाच । द्वे विद्ये वेदितव्ये इति ह स्म यदु ब्रह्मविदो वदन्ति
परा चैवापरा च ॥ १.१.४

tasmai sa hovāca | dve vidye veditavye iti ha sma yad
brahmavido vadanti parā caivāparā ca || 1.1.4

तस्मै सः ह उवाच । द्वे विद्ये वेदितव्ये इति ह स्म यत् ब्रह्मविदः वदन्ति
परा च एव अपरा च ॥

सः ^{m1/1} ह ⁰ तस्मै ^{m4/1} उवाच ^{iii/1 लिट्} ।

ब्रह्मविदः ^{m1/3} ह ⁰ द्वे ^{f2/1} विद्ये ^{f2/1} वेदितव्ये ^{तव्यत् n7/1} वदन्ति ^{iii/3 लट्}
।

यत् ^{n1/1} स्म ⁰ परा ^{f1/1} च ⁰ अपरा ^{f1/1} च ⁰ एव ⁰, इति ⁰ ॥

1.1.4 To him he thus replied, "The knowers of the Brahman or the enlightened Masters have spoken of two paths to liberation. परा the path of gyana yoga, and अपरा the path of karma yoga. And both these paths are within each other, परा चैवापरा च, both these paths are to be followed simultaneously".

The Body needs a discipline of waking, eating, working, exercising, entertainment and rest. The mind needs a discipline of sadhana and satsang. Both are necessary. Both go together and are a perfect match.

Regularly one needs to visit Guruji and spend time in his satsang, meditation, discourse and seva. So also one needs to perform one's responsibilities and chores with honesty and dedication.

TIME-SPACE or BODY-MIND are a continuum. Name_&_Form or Sound_&_Light both make up this Duality and harmonizing both leads to Advaita.

Subject and Object, Emotions and Sensations, Theory and Practice, Phonons and Photons, Matter and Energy, both are to be well-understood and judiciously applied.

तत्रापरा ऋग्वेदो यजुर्वेदः सामवेदोऽथर्ववेदः शिक्षा कल्पो व्याकरणं निरुक्तं छन्दो ज्योतिषमिति । अथ परा यया तदक्षरमधिगम्यते ॥ १.१.५

tatrāparā ṛgvedo yajurvedaḥ sāmavedo'tharvavedaḥ śikṣā kalpo vyākaraṇaṃ niruktaṃ chando jyotiṣamiti | atha parā yayā tadakṣaramadhigamyate || 1.1.5

तत्र अपरा ऋग्वेदः यजुर्वेदः सामवेदः अथर्ववेदः शिक्षा कल्पः व्याकरणं निरुक्तं छन्दः ज्योतिषम् इति । अथ परा यया तत् अक्षरम् अधिगम्यते ॥

तत्र ^{0} अपरा $^{f1/1}$ ऋग्वेदः $^{m1/1}$ यजुर्वेदः $^{m1/1}$ सामवेदः $^{m1/1}$ अथर्ववेदः $^{m1/1}$ शिक्षा $^{f1/1}$ कल्पः $^{m1/1}$ व्याकरणं $^{n1/1}$ निरुक्तं $^{n1/1}$ छन्दः $^{m1/1}$ ज्योतिषम् $^{n1/1}$, इति ^{0} ।
अथ ^{0} परा $^{f1/1}$ यया $^{f3/1}$ तत् $^{n2/1}$ अक्षरम् $^{n2/1}$ अधिगम्यते $^{iii/1}$ लट् कर्म० ॥

1.1.5 The Karma Yoga or अपरा विद्या is fully detailed in the four Vedas, viz. Rigveda, Yajurveda, Samaveda, Atharvaveda; and the six Upavedas, viz. Shiksha, Kalpa, Vyakarana, Nirukta, Chhandas and Jyotisha.

The Gyana Yoga or परा विद्या is the one by which Immortality is realized.

All of us go to school, then find work and raise a family. It is the process of Karma Yoga, doing what is right at that point in life, and moving forward. Simultaneously we seek to be at ease in the heart, resolving emotions, digesting thoughts, and keeping our innocence and purity intact. Initially when we are young, the Gyana Yoga is deeply ingrained and keeps working in parallel. As we get more colored or discolored by the vagaries of nature and society, the Gyana Yoga takes a back seat or is simply pushed under the carpet.

Then a day comes when Guruji (the Master or Divinity) comes in one's life. He lovingly takes one's hand and reestablishes one's balance. Then one can say Gyana Yoga has re-ignited.

This process may start at some definite point in life that is different for each one of us, and that is normal. Only the Seeker Finds. But what or who catalyzes one's seeking is hard to say. It is not written in any textbook nor taught in any school.

That is what Angiras means when he says अथ परा यया तद् अक्षरम् अधिगम्यते ।

One may have started to balance Time and Resources, one's wealth might have shown a steady Climb, one's fame might have sky-rocketed,
BUT peace in the heart is another ball game!

Immortality does not mean gaining an imperishable body or having immeasurable resources. Liberation does not mean living in a free country, getting desires fulfilled, or doing as one pleases. It cannot be succinctly put in words, but deep within, the heart knows it fully well. After all, it is in one's experience solidly as a baby or a youngster, then it starts to liquefy and by adult-hood it has become gaseous. Fitness is exactly what one is seeking, but until the time one stops, listens and asks the Guru, it is never addressed.

Like a sapling, the Guru's advice is also to be nurtured and assimilated bit by bit, so that faith and dispassion get firmly rooted within. Give it Time, give it Space, give it your very best shot.

यत् तदद्रेश्यमग्राह्यमगोत्रमवर्णमचक्षुःश्रोत्रं तदपाणिपादम् । नित्यं विभुं सर्वगतं सुसूक्ष्मं तदव्ययं यद् भूतयोनिं परिपश्यन्ति धीराः ॥ १.१.६

yat tad-adreśyam-agrāhyam-agotram-avarṇam-

acakṣuḥśrotraṃ tadapāṇipādam | nityaṃ vibhuṃ

sarvagataṃ susūkṣmaṃ tadavyayaṃ yad bhūtayoniṃ

paripaśyanti dhīrāḥ || 1.1.6

Now the verse that gives the essence of Gyana Yoga and lays the foundation for stepping into the vast Unknown that is also known as Freedom.

1.1.6 Wisdom is not contained in the sensory perceptions.

Wisdom is something different from that
- which can be seen अद्रैश्यम्
- which can be grasped, handled or addressed अग्राह्यम्
- which can be given any source attribute or genetic connotation अगोत्रम्
- which has any flavor or shade or distinct feature अवर्णम्
- which has organs noticed in mammals अचक्षुःश्रोत्रम् अपाणिपादं viz. eye ear hands feet, i.e. Wisdom is one that remains calm and at ease.

Wisdom is that which can be said
- to be continuous or eternal in Time नित्यं
- to be all that everyone perceives or realizes; or It is every known and unknown object, whether living or dead, whether animate or inanimate विभुं
- to be present in everything or all-pervading in Space सर्वगऽतं
- to be Wonderfully sublime, fine yet beautiful, small yet having a great impact सुसूक्ष्मं
- to maintain Itself without any change अव्ययं (due to circumstance, natural phenomenon, person,

place, time or situation).

Wisdom is that which the brave and the intelligent धीराः endowed with discrimination and detachment have परिपश्यन्ति realized भूतयोनिं Internally.

i.e.

There is no proof that Wisdom will show on anyone's forehead or in his skin color or in his religious beliefs or in his character or behavior or ...

i.e.

Saintliness is elusive both for the Subject and the Object. भूतयोनिं परिपश्यन्ति It is an Internal or Hidden talent, and It has the capacity to manifest in any being.

यथोर्णनाभिः सृजते गृह्णते च यथा पृथिव्यामोषधयः सम्भवन्ति । यथा सतः पुरुषात् केशलोमानि तथाऽक्षरात् सम्भवतीह विश्वम् ॥ १.१.७
yathorṇanābhiḥ sṛjate gṛhṇate ca yathā pṛthivyām-
oṣadhayaḥ sambhavanti | yathā sataḥ puruṣāt keśalomāni
tathā'kṣarāt sambhavatīha viśvam ॥ 1.1.7

यथा उर्णनाभिः सृजते गृह्णते च यथा पृथिव्याम् ओषधयः सम्भवन्ति ।
यथा सतः पुरुषात् केशलोमानि तथा अक्षरात् सम्भवति इह विश्वम् ॥

$1.1.7$ The Guru gives some practical examples to illustrate the point further.

1.7.1 As a spider weaves is web, and also swallows it from time to time यथोर्णनाभिः सृजते गृह्णते

1.7.2 As deliciousNutritiousHealing herbs from the soil sprout यथा पृथिव्याम् ओषधयः संभवन्ति

1.7.3 As on living men hair grow spontaneously on head and skin यथा सतः पुरुषात् केशलोमानि

1.7.4 Similarly it is all Happening in the world तथा इह अक्षरात् विश्वम् सम्भवति spiraling from the V A S T Infinite.

There is a logic somewhere, yet most of it is beyond logic. Some things can be reasoned out, yet the majority is beyond reason. Seemingly the plants and animals and machines seem to have a fixed design, but the men who create machines and nature that creates flora is unpredictable.
Don't stop, Just Drop, and move on.

The Guru is giving an inkling of the Mahavakya - कुछ जान के चलो कुछ मान के चलो, सब को प्रेम से गले लगा के चलो । Walk lightly as a cloud, be humble as the grass.

And now the Master is indicating the means thereby.

तपसा चीयते ब्रह्म ततोऽन्नमभिजायते ।

अन्नात् प्राणो मनः सत्यं लोकाः कर्मसु चामृतम् ॥ १.१.८

tapasā cīyate brahma tato'nnamabhijāyate | annāt prāṇo
manaḥ satyaṃ lokāḥ karmasu cāmṛtam ‖ 1.1.8

तपसा चीयते ब्रह्म ततः अन्नम् अभिजायते ।

अन्नात् प्राणः मनः सत्यं लोकाः कर्मसु च अमृतम् ॥

ब्रह्म $^{n1/1}$ तपसा $^{n3/1}$ चीयते $^{iii/1}$ लट् ,

ततः ^{0} अन्नम् $^{n1/1}$ अभिजायते $^{iii/1}$ लट् ।

अन्नात् $^{n5/1}$ प्राणः $^{m1/1}$ मनः $^{n1/1}$ सत्यं $^{n1/1}$ लोकाः $^{m1/3}$ च ^{0},

कर्मसु $^{n7/1}$ अमृतम् $^{n1/1}$ ॥

1.1.8 Energy, Strength and Stamina ब्रह्म are the result चीयते of good discipline and long-term practice तपसा. Tapas is also related to gainful employment since without that no divine activity can be envisioned. Thereby ततः skill is got and food अन्नम् can be grown, eaten and digested अभिजायते.

With proper nutrition अन्नात् , the life force प्राणः is sustained, the mind and intellect मनः function well, and Truth सत्यं prevails in life i.e. in the three worlds लोकाः inner heart, outer environment, close by subtle currents.

Thence तथा is derived the mastery over one's desires अमृतं. Only then can our expectations be properly met and our aspirations fulfilled अमृतं. This is called the Law of Karma कर्मसु or the cycle of human evolution.

यः सर्वज्ञः सर्वविद् यस्य ज्ञानमयं तपः ।

तस्मादेतद् ब्रह्म नाम रूपमन्नं च जायते ॥ १.१.९

yaḥ sarvajñaḥ sarvavid yasya jñānamayaṃ tapaḥ |

tasmādetad brahma nāma rūpamannaṃ ca jāyate ‖ 1.1.9

यः सर्वज्ञः सर्वविद् यस्य ज्ञानमयं तपः ।

तस्मात् एतत् ब्रह्म नाम रूपम् अन्नं च जायते ॥

यः $^{m1/1}$ सर्वज्ञः $^{m1/1}$ सर्वविद् $^{m1/1}$ यस्य $^{n6/1}$ ज्ञानमयं $^{PPPn1/1}$ तपः $^{n2/1}$ ।

तस्मात् $^{n5/1}$ एतत् $^{n1/1}$ ब्रह्म $^{n1/1}$ नाम $^{n1/1}$ रूपम् $^{n1/1}$ अन्नं $^{n1/1}$ च $^{n1/1}$ जायते $^{iii/1}$ लट् ॥

1.1.9 The One who यः is omniscient all-knowing सर्वज्ञः and has a deeper understanding सर्वविद् of all laws. The One whose यस्य fire of discipline burns bright, whose lamp of wisdom ज्ञानमयं तपः is lit,

From that One तस्माद् , this एतद् big creation ब्रह्म , this V A S T nation नाम , corporation रूपम् , and galactic matter अन्नं is produced जायाते and sustained.

Obviously to run a multi-billion dollar empire a multi-faceted skill-set, enormous stamina, and an inventive mind are needed.

To rule over a nation, a high degree of resourcefulness, abundance of soft-skills and boundless energy are the key. Only then the cycle of peaceful growth and effervescent evolution are shaped.

Here ends the first part of the teaching. Close of the first semester of the first year of a three year university degree program. 12:57pm 9.1.20 Jai Gurudev.

1st Year 2nd Semester

The student has survived the first term, in fact has done quite well, and is hopeful of finishing the first year on a high note.

The Master senses the enthusiasm and starts a new chapter of unlimited possibilities for the student.

Now begins the second part or the second semester.

The Master advises to refresh all that was taught earlier. Then he begins to talk on the practical aspects that will help in living to the best of one's abilities.

The principal topic is Praise for becoming rich and famous in the world, at the same time not let the heart be carried away and imprisoned by the entanglements and attractions.

Mundaka is highlighting the fate of the great souls. On one hand the famous can retain their goodwill and live till the end unstained and pure. On the other hand they can lose their balance and become embroiled in the storms of impure relationships and dealings.

The Laws of Motion

These are practical aspects of the laws of creation, also known as the plane of birth and death. This is the plane of human birth.

It is the karmic plane where the classical laws of Newtonian mechanics hold good:
1) Every object persists in its state of rest or uniform motion in a straight line unless it is compelled to change that state by an external force acting on it.
2) Force equals Mass times Acceleration.
3) For every action there is an equal and opposite reaction.

Restated
1) Law of Inertia
2) Law of Growth
3) Law of Conservation of Momentum

Later on, when the student clears the initial exams, the quantum mechanics and physics is explained, where respect rules, love is supreme.

तदेतत् सत्यं मन्त्रेषु कर्माणि कवयो यान्यपश्यंस्तानि त्रेतायां बहुधा सन्ततानि । तान्याचरथ नियतं सत्यकामा एष वः पन्थाः सुकृतस्य लोके ॥ १.२.१

tadetat satyam mantreṣu karmāṇi kavayo yānyapaśyaṃstāni tretāyāṃ bahudhā santatāni | tānyācaratha niyataṃ satyakāmā eṣa vaḥ panthāḥ sukṛtasya loke ॥ 1.2.1

तत् एतत् सत्यं मन्त्रेषु कर्माणि कवयः यानि अपश्यन् तानि त्रेतायां बहुधा सन्ततानि । तानि आचरथ नियतं सत्यकामाः एषः वः पन्थाः सुकृतस्य लोके ॥

तत् $^{n1/1}$ एतत् $^{n1/1}$ सत्यं $^{n1/1}$,
मन्त्रेषु $^{m7/3}$ कवयः $^{m1/3}$ कर्माणि $^{n2/3}$ यानि $^{n2/3}$ अपश्यन् $^{iii/3\, लङ्}$,
त्रेतायां $^{f7/1}$ बहुधा ^{0} तानि $^{n2/3}$ सन्ततानि $^{PPPn1/3}$ ।
सत्यकामाः $^{m1/3}$ वः $^{mfn2/3}$ तानि $^{n2/3}$ नियतं $^{m2/1}$ आचरथ $^{ii/3\, लट्}$,
एषः $^{m1/1}$ पन्थाः $^{m1/1}$ सुकृतस्य $^{m6/1}$ लोके $^{m7/1}$ ॥

1.2.1 This is the whole truth of the matter. This that has been taught in the last semester is the exact blueprint of life lived in the Treta - The age between 50 and 75 years when man is most experienced, broad-minded and useful to society at large.

तदेतत् सत्यं मन्त्रेषु कर्माणि कवयो यान्यपश्यंस्तानि त्रेतायां बहुधा संततानि।

Satyuga = Brahmacarya = Pure Childhood = 0 to 25.
Dvapar = Grihasta = all focus on earning = 25 to 50.
Treta = Vanprastha = endowed with viveka, vairagya, titiksha, uparati = 50 to 75 years.
Kalyuga = Sannyasa = again with a childlike mind but worn out body = 75 to 100 years.

Learn well and assimilate perfectly, so that you also walk the path as the heroes of yore. Just as the great men did it earlier, so shall you also live a life of beauty, charm, creativity, prosperity and happiness.

तान्याचरथ नियतं सत्यकामा एष वः पन्थाः सुकृतस्य लोके ॥

Learn from Virat Kohli, from Kane Williamson, from Jasprit Bumrah, from your chosen idol. Ingrain the teachings well. Go out and play, may your performance be splendid.

यदा लेलायते ह्यर्चिः समिद्धे हव्यवाहने ।
तदाज्यभागावन्तरेणाहुतीः प्रतिपादयेत् ॥ १.२.२

yadā lelāyate hyarciḥ samiddhe havyavāhane |
tadājyabhāgāvantareṇāhutīḥ pratipādayet || 1.2.2

यदा लेलायते ह अर्चिः समिद्धे हव्यवाहने ।
तदा आज्यभागौ अन्तरेण आहुतीः प्रतिपादयेत् ॥

यदा ^{0} ह ^{0} समिद्धे $^{m7/1}$ हव्यवाहने $^{m7/1}$ अर्चिः $^{m1/1}$ लेलायते $^{iii/1}$ लट्
। तदा ^{0} आज्यभागौ $^{m2/2}$ अन्तरेण ^{0} आहुतीः $^{f2/3}$ प्रतिपादयेत्
$^{iii/1}$ विधि लिङ् ॥

1.2.2 When nature is conducive, when the weather is bright and sunny, when the Gods are benevolent, when your mood is balanced, that is the time to reach out, work hard and go the extra mile.

Action is enjoined when the situation is ripe. In a Yagya, slowly stoke up the flames by pouring ghee in the correct space. That is an art. To maintain peak performance, lots of discipline and regular workouts are needed.

Do your efforts in tune to the need of the hour.

Time your strokes and stretches in accordance with the flexibility of your limbs. Make hay while the sun shines. Approach the administrator when his mood is conducive. Stock up in winter. Use an umbrella in the rainy season.

Now how to prevent a major fault, avoid unforced error, and not get into reckless living are taught.

यस्याग्निहोत्रमदर्शमपौर्णमासमचातुर्मास्यमनाग्रयणमतिथिवर्जितं च ।
अहुतमवैश्वदेवमविधिना हुतमासप्तमांस्तस्य लोकान् हिनस्ति ॥ १.२.३

yasyāgnihotramadarśamapaurṇamāsamacāturmāsyamanā
grayaṇamatithivarjitaṃ ca |
ahutamavaiśvadevamavidhinā hutamāsaptamāṃstasya
lokān hinasti ‖ 1.2.3

यस्य अग्निहोत्रम् अदर्शम् अपौर्णमासम् अचातुर्मास्यम् अनाग्रयणम्
अतिथिवर्जितं च । अहुतम् अवैश्वदेवम् अविधिना हुतम् आसप्तमान्
तस्य लोकान् हिनस्ति ॥

यस्य $^{m6/1}$ अविधिना $^{m3/1}$ अग्निहोत्रम् $^{m2/1}$ अदर्शम् $^{m2/1}$
अपौर्णमासम् $^{m2/1}$ अचातुर्मास्यम् $^{m2/1}$ अनाग्रयणम् $^{m2/1}$
अतिथिवर्जितं $^{m2/1}$ अहुतम् $^{PPPn2/1}$ अवैश्वदेवम् $^{m2/1}$ च ^{0} हुतम्
$^{PPPn1/1}$
,
तस्य $^{m6/1}$ आसप्तमान् $^{m2/3}$ लोकान् $^{m2/3}$ हिनस्ति $^{iii/1}$ लट् ॥

1.2.3 Perform your task as advised and learnt, and be punctual and practice cleanliness. Only a few things can be done spontaneously, in the long run life should be lived with proper planning, mediation and preparation.

Some tasks need to be attended to daily अग्निहोत्रम्, like our morning chores and rituals. Do not skip them.

Some tasks need to be carried out to the letter अदर्शम्, strictly as per design, so do not miss any intermediate step. Like cooking or tea making or bank account opening or income tax filing, for such chores just follow the format without being too inventive.

Some tasks are fortnightly or monthly, like paying the bills, getting the salary, going for a sauna or pancakarma, etc. अपौर्णमासम् no need to postpone or prepone these activities.

Some activities are dependent on the season like summer, monsoon, winter, so be not misaligned to that अचातुर्मास्यम्, rather be blessed that a change has come and cheerfully acknowledge the same.

Festivals and Celebrations and Birthday parties certainly cannot be given the cold-shoulder by not inviting guests and friends अतिथिवर्जितम्, or you shall find your relationships muddled and society shall look down upon you.

Be appropriate in attending to the needs of individual family members, and in dealing with various colleagues and staff and the boss at work. You must not behave in the same manner with the Guru as you behave with the devotees.
अहुतम् अवैश्वदेवम् अविधिना हुतम् - in the army adhere to the military commandments, do not be official at home or vice versa.

Else your entire family and successors shall get tainted and suffer the backlash of faulty conduct.
तस्य आसप्तमान् लोकान् हिनस्ति

काली कराली च मनोजवा च सुलोहिता या च सुधूम्रवर्णा ।
स्फुलिङ्गिनी विश्वरुची च देवी लेलायमाना इति सप्त जिह्वाः ॥ १.२.४
kālī karālī ca manojavā ca sulohitā yā ca sudhūmravarṇā |
sphuliṅginī viśvarucī ca devī lelāyamānā iti sapta jihvāḥ ॥
1.2.4

काली कराली च मनोजवा च सुलोहिता या च सुधूम्रवर्णा ।
स्फुलिङ्गिनी विश्वरुची च देवी लेलायमानाः इति सप्त जिह्वाः ॥

या [f1/1] काली [f1/1] कराली [f1/1] च [0] मनोजवा [f1/1] च [0] सुलोहिता [f1/1] च [0] सुधूम्रवर्णा [f1/1] स्फुलिङ्गिनी [f1/1] विश्वरुची [f1/1] देवी [f1/1] च [0] ,
इति [0] सप्त [mfn1/3] लेलायमानाः [f1/3] जिह्वाः [f1/3] ॥

1.2.4 Seven milestones in the human journey - birth, yagyopavit, university, marriage, job, raising a family, and liberation. Seven are the chakras from mooladhara to sahasrara. Seven seas and seven continents constitute the planet earth. Seven colors of the rainbow and seven notes in the musical octave and seven days of the week. In the Puranas, the Sun-God is described as riding a chariot drawn by seven horses.

Each milestone is likened to a bright flame that makes life go forward. Lighting the way and inspiring and propelling as well. Names of the milestone flames have been given to add grace, lend charm and be easily memorized. Just as in school so many rote items are given a catchy phrase.

काली = fragrant = sense alluring, कराली = lines on the palm = design template, मनोजवा = fast as the mind, सुलोहिता = deep red = enthusiastic, सुधूम्रवर्णा = deep gray = serious, स्फुलिङ्गिनी = dancing figure, विश्वरुची = dazzling, देवी = most beautiful

---

Rewards of shouldering responsibility are stated in the next few verses.

एतेषु यश्चरते भ्राजमानेषु यथाकालं चाहुतयो ह्याददायन् ।

तं नयन्त्येताः सूर्यस्य रश्मयो यत्र देवानां पतिरेकोऽधिवासः ॥ १.२.५

eteṣu yaścarate bhrājamāneṣu yathākālaṃ cāhutayo

hyādadāyan | taṃ nayantyetāḥ sūryasya raśmayo yatra

devānāṃ patireko'dhivāsaḥ || 1.2.5

एतेषु यः चरते भ्राजमानेषु यथाकालं च आहुतयः हि आददायन् ।

तं नयन्ति एताः सूर्यस्य रश्मयः यत्र देवानां पतिः एकः अधिवासः ॥

यः ^{m1/1} हि ⁰ एतेषु ^{m7/3} भ्राजमानेषु ^{f7/3} यथाकालं ^{m2/1} च ⁰ चरते

^{iii/1 लट्} , एताः ^{f1/3} आहुतयः ^{f1/3} आददायन् ^{iii/3 लङ्} ।

सूर्यस्य ^{m6/1} रश्मयः ^{m1/3} तं ^{m2/1} नयन्ति ^{iii/3} ,

यत्र ⁰ देवानां ^{m6/3} एकः ^{m1/1} पतिः ^{m1/1} अधिवासः ^{m1/1} ॥

एह्येहीति तमाहुतयः सुवर्चसः सूर्यस्य रश्मिभिर्यजमानं वहन्ति ।

प्रियां वाचमभिवदन्त्योऽर्चयन्त्य एष वः पुण्यः सुकृतो ब्रह्मलोकः ॥ ६

ehyehīti tamāhutayaḥ suvarcasaḥ sūryasya

raśmibhiryajamānaṃ vahanti |

priyāṃ vācamabhivadantyo'rcayantya eṣa vaḥ puṇyaḥ

sukṛto brahmalokaḥ || 1.2.6

एहि एहि इति तम् आहुतयः सुवर्चसः सूर्यस्य रश्मिभिः यजमानं

वहन्ति । प्रियां वाचम् अभिवदन्त्यः अर्चयन्त्यः एषः वः पुण्यः

सुकृतः ब्रह्मलोकः ॥

एहि ^{ii/1 लोट्} एहि ^{ii/1 लोट्} , इति ⁰ ।

प्रियां ^{f2/1} वाचम् ^{f2/1} अभिवदन्त्यः ^{f1/3 शतृ} अर्चयन्त्यः ^{f1/3 शतृ} ,

एषः ^{m1/1} पुण्यः ^{m1/1} ब्रह्मलोकः ^{m1/1} वः ^{mfn2/3} सुकृतः ^{PPPm1/1} ,

सुवर्चसः ^{f1/3} आहुतयः ^{f1/3} सूर्यस्य ^{m6/1} रश्मिभिः ^{m3/3} तम् ^{m2/1}

यजमानं ^{m2/1} वहन्ति ^{iii/3 लट्} ॥

1.2.5 To the one who is regular in performance of duty, honest and earnest and gives painstaking attention to every detail; such a one easily climbs the ladder to the top. His merit is amply rewarded, there is phenomenal increase in his responsibilities, and he quickly ascends to the highest post.

1.2.6 Success beckons, fame nudges, society kisses, divinity takes him by the hand. He is given a red-carpet welcome wherever he goes, and accorded a high seat of honor.

Now, words of caution to prevent the seeker from stumbling or falling.

प्लवा ह्येते अदृढा यज्ञरूपा अष्टादशोक्तमवरं येषु कर्म ।
एतच्छ्रेयो येऽभिनन्दन्ति मूढा जरामृत्युं ते पुनरेवापि यन्ति ॥ १.२.७

plavā hyete adṛḍhā yajñarūpā aṣṭādaśoktamavaraṃ yeṣu
karma | etacchreyo ye'bhinandanti mūḍhā jarāmṛtyuṃ te
punarevāpi yanti || 1.2.7

प्लवाः हि एते अदृढाः यज्ञरूपाः अष्टादशः उक्तम् अवरं येषु कर्म ।
एतत् श्रेयः ये अभिनन्दन्ति मूढाः जरामृत्युं ते पुनः एव अपि यन्ति ॥

एते$^{m1/3}$ हि^{0} अदृढाः$^{m1/3}$ प्लवाः$^{m1/3}$ अष्टादशः$^{m1/3}$ यज्ञरूपाः$^{m1/3}$
येषु$^{m7/3}$ अवरं$^{n1/1}$ कर्म$^{n1/1}$ उक्तम्$^{PPPn1/1}$ ।
ये$^{m1/3}$ मूढाः$^{m1/3}$ एतत्$^{n2/1}$ श्रेयः$^{n2/1}$ अभिनन्दन्ति$^{iii/3}$ लट् ,
ते$^{m1/3}$ पुनः^{0} अपि^{0} जरामृत्युं$^{m2/1}$ एव^0 यन्ति$^{iii/3}$ लट् ॥

1.2.7 These eighteen virtues, tools or skills are highly prized by the lay public, particularly by the media, also known as the fourth estate.

However it is not enough to rise outwardly. If the inner Being is not listened to or properly addressed, then name and fame and wealth and glory come to naught. Their transient nature gets revealed soon enough. One must not get stuck in the outer.

One must never stop toiling even after attaining purity of thought. One must not give up humility, punctuality, innocence and belongingness.

The ego of righteousness, or the ego of a successful man is a dangerous pitfall. Such an ego can destroy all merit in the twinkling of an eye.

अविद्यायामन्तरे वर्तमानाः स्वयं धीराः पण्डितं मन्यमानाः ।
जङ्घन्यमानाः परियन्ति मूढा अन्धेनैव नीयमाना यथान्धाः ॥ १.२.८

avidyāyāmantare vartamānāḥ svayaṃ dhīrāḥ paṇḍitaṃ manyamānāḥ | jaṅghanyamānāḥ pariyanti mūḍhā andhenaiva nīyamānā yathāndhāḥ || 1.2.8

अविद्यायाम् अन्तरे वर्तमानाः स्वयं धीराः पण्डितं मन्यमानाः ।
जङ्घन्यमानाः परियन्ति मूढाः अन्धेन एव नीयमानाः यथा अन्धाः ॥

अविद्यायाम्[f7/1] अन्तरे[m7/1] वर्तमानाः[PrPA m1/3 शानच्] स्वयं[0] धीराः[m1/3] पण्डितं[m2/1] मन्यमानाः[PrPA m1/3 शानच्] । मूढाः[m1/3] जङ्घन्यमानाः[PrPA m1/3 शानच्] परियन्ति[iii/3] , यथा[0] अन्धाः[m1/3] नीयमानाः[PrPA m1/3 शानच्] अन्धेन[m3/1] एव[0] ॥

1.2.8 Like the blind led by the blind, a scientist or professor or infatuated artist or high official or successful businessman can succumb to this dangerous ego and get trapped. His evolution then stops, and his decline begins.

His foolish company might keep him in raptures of delight, but there are wicked storms waiting to cause his ruin by and by.

Peace in the heart and clarity in the mind are adversely affected by fame and wealth - this golden principle is stated boldly.

अविद्यायां बहुधा वर्तमाना वयं कृतार्था इत्यभिमन्यन्ति बालाः ।
यत् कर्मिणो न प्रवेदयन्ति रागात् तेनातुराः क्षीणलोकाश्च्यवन्ते ॥ ९

avidyāyāṃ bahudhā vartamānā vayaṃ kṛtārthā
ityabhimanyanti bālāḥ | yat karmiṇo na pravedayanti rāgāt
tenāturāḥ kṣīṇalokāścyavante ॥ 1.2.9

अविद्यायां बहुधा वर्तमानाः वयं कृतार्थाः इति अभिमन्यन्ति बालाः ।
यत् कर्मिणः न प्रवेदयन्ति रागात् तेन आतुराः क्षीणलोकाः च्यवन्ते ॥

अविद्यायां[f7/1] बहुधा[0] वर्तमानाः[PrPA m1/3] वयं[m1/3] बालाः[m1/3]
कृतार्थाः[m1/3] , इति[0] अभिमन्यन्ति[iii/3] ।
यत्[0] कर्मिणः[m1/3] रागात्[m5/1] न[0] प्रवेदयन्ति[iii/3 लट्] ,
आतुराः[m1/3] क्षीणलोकाः[m1/3] तेन[m3/1] च्यवन्ते[iii/3 लट्] ॥

46

1.2.9 Ignorance stalks those riding the foolish winds of worldly glory. Ignorance gnaws at the heart and shrouds all wisdom.

The wheel turns full circle and one is thrown to the bottom of the ladder again. This is a big mystery, and bigger still is that so many popular people bite the dust in the end.

Then there is no way out, since
- the body has lost its youthful charm,
- the mind has lost its suppleness, and
- the intellect no longer knows how to surrender, being shackled by dizzying memories.

इष्टापूर्तं मन्यमाना वरिष्ठं नान्यच्छ्रेयो वेदयन्ते प्रमूढाः ।
नाकस्य पृष्ठे ते सुकृतेऽनुभूत्वेमं लोकं हीनतरं वा विशन्ति ॥ १.२.१०

iṣṭāpūrtaṃ manyamānā variṣṭham nānyacchreyo
vedayante pramūḍhāḥ | nākasya pṛṣṭhe te

sukṛte'nubhūtvemaṃ lokaṃ hīnataraṃ vā viśanti ॥ 1.2.10

इष्टापूर्तं मन्यमानाः वरिष्ठं न अन्यत् श्रेयः वेदयन्ते प्रमूढाः ।
नाकस्य पृष्ठे ते सुकृते अनुभूत्वा इमं लोकं हीनतरं वा विशन्ति ॥

वरिष्ठं $^{n2/1}$ इष्टापूर्तं $^{n2/1}$ मन्यमानाः $^{PrPA\ 1/3}$ शानच् ,
प्रमूढाः $^{m1/3}$ अन्यत् ^{0} श्रेयः $^{n2/1}$ न ^{0} वेदयन्ते $^{iii/3}$ लट् ।
सुकृते $^{n7/1}$ due to merits अनुभूत्वा ^{0} क्त्वा having enjoyed, ते
$^{m1/3}$ they नाकस्य $^{n6/1}$ of heavenly पृष्ठे $^{n7/1}$ regions इमं
$^{m2/1}$ this लोकं $^{m2/1}$ world विशन्ति $^{iii/3}$ लट् enter, हीनतरं
$^{m2/1}$ वा ^{0} or the clueless ॥

1.2.10 Bodily illness and emotional friction in relationships makes their life miserable in old age, the years from 75 to 100 are also called Kalyuga.

Based on intellectual deeds devoid of divine vision, in old age they may lead a life not wishing for anything better, or even be subject to a clueless survival.

An important point.
The Upanishad is not talking about fantasy, dream, or improbable after life goodies. It is boldly stating the practical, here and now in this lifetime.

<u>Babyhood to OldAge alone is outlined</u>.
(some commentators interpret it as after life, no matter since it is well within the 400 year span).

तपःश्रद्धे ये ह्युपवसन्त्यरण्ये शान्ता विद्वांसो भैक्ष्यचर्यां चरन्तः ।
सूर्यद्वारेण ते विरजाः प्रयान्ति यत्रामृतः स पुरुषो ह्यव्ययात्मा ॥ ११

tapaḥśraddhe ye hyupavasantyaraṇye śāntā vidvāṃso
bhaikṣyacaryāṃ carantaḥ | sūryadvāreṇa te virajāḥ
prayānti yatrāmṛtaḥ sa puruṣo hyavyayātmā ‖ 1.2.11

तपःश्रद्धे ये हि उपवसन्ति अरण्ये शान्ताः विद्वांसः भैक्ष्यचर्यां चरन्तः ।
सूर्यद्वारेण ते विरजाः प्रयान्ति यत्र अमृतः सः पुरुषः हि अव्ययात्मा ॥

तपःश्रद्धे $^{m7/1}$ हि ^{0} अरण्ये $^{n7/1}$ ये $^{m1/3}$ उपवसन्ति $^{iii/3}$ लट् ,
शान्ताः $^{m1/3}$ विद्वांसः $^{m1/3}$ भैक्ष्यचर्यां $^{f2/1}$ चरन्तः $^{PrPA\ m1/3}$ शतृ ।
ते $^{m1/3}$ विरजाः $^{m1/3}$ सूर्यद्वारेण $^{m3/1}$ प्रयान्ति $^{iii/3}$,
यत्र ^{0} हि ^{0} सः $^{m1/1}$ अमृतः $^{m1/1}$ पुरुषः $^{m1/1}$ अव्ययात्मा $^{m1/1}$ ॥

1.2.11 On the other hand Sannyasa in that age is the golden time that comes to those engaged in tapas, austerity, surrender and devotion.

Maintain these simple living traits even after having reached the pinnacle, since then alone can the body and mind be safe-guarded in old age. And the heart kept blemish free.

Fear and worry cannot touch such souls. Illness too has no wickedness for them. Their life in old age is a harmony, being cleansed of all attachments, it is as if illumined by the gentle light of the sun.

If your old age is peaceful and filled with cheerful love and devotion, that is the highest attainment. This is stated as immortality in the scriptures.

परीक्ष्य लोकान् कर्मचितान् ब्राह्मणो निर्वेदमायान्नास्त्यकृतः कृतेन ।
तद्विज्ञानार्थं स गुरुमेवाभिगच्छेत् समित्पाणिः श्रोत्रियं ब्रह्मनिष्ठम् ॥ १२

parīkṣya lokān karmacitān
brāhmaṇornirvedamāyānnāstyakṛtaḥ kṛtena |
tadvijñānārtham sa gurumevābhigacchet samitpāṇiḥ
śrotriyam brahmaniṣṭham ॥ 1.2.12

परीक्ष्य लोकान् कर्मचितान् ब्राह्मणः निर्वेदम् आयात् न अस्ति अकृतः
कृतेन । तत् विज्ञानार्थं सः गुरुम् एव अभिगच्छेत् समित्पाणिः श्रोत्रियं
ब्रह्मनिष्ठम् ॥

परीक्ष्य $^{0\,ल्यप्}$ having experienced लोकान् $^{m2/3}$ the extent of social pleasures कर्मचितान् $^{m2/3}$ attainable through social standards ब्राह्मणः $^{m1/1}$ the discerning individual निर्वेदम् $^{m2/1}$ dispassionate आयात् $^{iii/1\,लङ्}$ got, तत् $^{n1/1}$ That अकृतः $^{m1/1}$ inner कृतेन $^{m3/1}$ by striving externally न ^{0} अस्ति $^{iii/1\,लट्}$ cannot be । समित्पाणिः $^{m1/1}$ with hands ready to serve सः $^{m1/1}$ he विज्ञानार्थं $^{m2/1}$ to acquire wisdom एव ^{0} only श्रोत्रियं $^{m2/1}$ one with a tradition and heritage ब्रह्मनिष्ठम् $^{m2/1}$ established in peaceful bliss गुरुम् $^{m2/1}$ Master अभिगच्छेत् $^{iii/1\,विधि\,लिङ्}$ should approach ॥

1.2.12 O Seeker! if thou art smart, if thou art intelligent, then in youth itself thou shalt take refuge in the Master.

In the prime of life you shall make it a priority to reach out to Guruji.

You shall not defer it till later. You shall seek the company and counsel of Wisdom. You shall attend satsang and become regular in sadhana and spiritual practices.

Yoga and Meditation shall form a tamper-proof part of your daily rituals. You shall serve the Master with a pure heart till the end.

तस्मै स विद्वानुपसन्नाय सम्यक् प्रशान्तचित्ताय शामान्विताय ।
येनाक्षरं पुरुषं वेद सत्यं प्रोवाच तां तत्त्वतो ब्रह्मविद्याम् ॥ १.२.१३
tasmai sa vidvānupasannāya samyak praśāntacittāya
śamānvitāya | yenākṣaraṃ puruṣaṃ veda satyaṃ provāca
tāṃ tattvato brahmavidyām ॥ 1.2.13

तस्मै सः विद्वान् उपसन्नाय सम्यक् प्रशान्तचित्ताय शामान्विताय ।
येन अक्षरं पुरुषं वेद सत्यं प्रोवाच तां तत्त्वतः ब्रह्मविद्याम् ॥

सः$^{m1/1}$ He विद्वान्$^{m1/1}$ the great Master तस्मै$^{m4/1}$ to him
उपसन्नाय$^{m4/1}$ to the one standing close प्रशान्तचित्ताय$^{m4/1}$
to the one with non-arguing intellect शामान्विताय$^{m4/1}$ to
the one with balanced lifestyle ,
येन$^{m3/1}$ by which सत्यं$^{m2/1}$ the true अक्षरं$^{m2/1}$ the infallible
पुरुषं$^{m2/1}$ goodness वेद$^{iii/1}$ लट् is known,
तां$^{f2/1}$ that ब्रह्मविद्याम्$^{f2/1}$ supreme knowledge सम्यक्^{0} in
great detail तत्त्वतः^{0} in practical form प्रोवाच$^{iii/1}$ लिट्
explained ॥

1.2.13 For such a soul is the veil of ignorance shattered. To him the Guru himself reveals the fount of wisdom. The divine makes the meeting certain. The highest knowledge is then imparted by the preceptor to the disciple.

Qualifications of the seeker are clearly stated.

1) Non-arguing intellect प्रशान्तचित्ताय । An employee or student or servant fits the bill when his nature is humble, ready to listen, willing to accept.

2) Having balance in lifestyle शमान्विताय । The student who is willing to work indoors as well as outdoors, who gives time to family, hobby, meditation, who has a discipline in eating and spending.

Method of Instruction is given clearly.

1) In great detail सम्यक् । Comprehensive and exhaustive treatment of the subject. Proper, complete, and fulfilling lectures.

2) In practical form तत्त्वतः । The highest skill cannot be imparted without real-life training. Hands-on projects, industry internships, and enough practice makes the man perfect.

2nd Year 1st Semester

Strangers, acquaintances, distant cousins, foreigners cannot go to that depths of nadir, since they have no emotion to drive it.

Conversely the charm of togetherness and beauty of bonding between two people is what Sparks off the greatest inventions, discoveries, entrepreneurships and enduring tales of mankind.

A wonderful story hinges on a superb cast. A great institution is forged by the teamwork of family members and partners.

This verse boldly says that all humans have much in common; and that can serve as an antidote and heal many relationships. Similarly it points to the undeniable fact that in the process of manufacturing (or birth) we unavoidably imbibe some distinct traits, which again is good for us. Then it goes on to mention the sameness of our death and departure. We all discard the body.

तदेतत् सत्यं यथा सुदीप्तात् पावकाद् विस्फुलिङ्गाः सहस्रशः प्रभवन्ते सरूपाः । तथाऽक्षराद् विविधाः सोम्य भावाः प्रजायन्ते तत्र चैवापि यन्ति ॥ २.१.१

tadetat satyaṃ yathā sudīptāt pāvakād visphuliṅgāḥ sahasraśaḥ prabhavante sarūpāḥ | tathā'kṣarād vividhāḥ somya bhāvāḥ prajāyante tatra caivāpi yanti ॥ 2.1.1

2.1.1 Everything is born from the One. From one sun countless rays reach every nook and corner of our planet. From the fire in our hearth brilliant sparks keep us warm as those from the *Lohri* bonfire. All of us drink water from the regular rains, from oceans, lakes and rivers. And we all breathe the same oxygen and eat the grain grown by the same farmer.

An entire village gets populated from the union of a couple.

Now why is this verse so important? What is it trying to convey? And how does that help in our daily life?

Firstly it tells us to strongly etch the fact that we are all from the same stock. We are all made up of the same thing. We all have the same core, the disparity is superficial.

This fact is a big relief. This idea is a great leveler of ego. It can erase bitterness and make us equanimous, productive, and creative on a large scale that is the result of strong teamwork.

This verse also highlights another poignant reality. Maximum hate, conflict and destruction can only occur between family members - Father and Son, Brother and Brother. Or between two married people or between close friends.

दिव्यो ह्यमूर्तः पुरुषः सबाह्याभ्यन्तरो ह्यजः ।
अप्राणो ह्यमनाः शुभ्रो ह्यक्षरात् परतः परः ॥ २.१.२

divyo hyamūrtaḥ puruṣaḥ sa bāhyābhyantaro hyajaḥ |
aprāṇo hyamanāḥ śubhro hyakṣarāt parataḥ paraḥ ॥ 2.1.2

दिव्यः हि अमूर्तः पुरुषः सबाह्याभ्यन्तरः हि अजः ।
अप्राणः हि अमनाः शुभ्रः हि अक्षरात् परतः परः ॥

दिव्यः[m1/1] हि[0] अमूर्तः[m1/1] पुरुषः[m1/1] सबाह्याभ्यन्तरः[m1/1] हि[0] अजः[m1/1] , अप्राणः[m1/1] हि[0] अमनाः[m1/1] शुभ्रः[m1/1] हि[0] , अक्षरात्[m5/1] परतः[0] परः[m1/1] ॥

$2.1.2$ Brahman पुरुषः is thought of as luminous दिव्यः, formless अमूर्तं, all pervading सबाह्याभ्यन्तरः, unborn अजः, benevolent शुभ्रः, not requiring sustenance अप्राणः, not requiring decision making अमनाः, from the eternal अक्षरात्, beyond all परतः lofty परः imagination.

The imagination of the seer stretches far. The divine is honored in the most exalted ways. The sky's the limit. To achieve anything grand, aim for the stars.

Goodness has no parallel. It has no compromises. No adjustments, shortcuts, half-hearted attempts. No rush, no hurry, no tension.

There is an abundance. It is enough. All can be taken care of. None is left un-provided for. Nothing comes in the way. No hurdles, jams, nor any conflicts.

एतस्माज्जायते प्राणो मनः सर्वेन्द्रियाणि च ।

खं वायुज्र्यौतिरापः पृथिवी विश्वस्य धारिणी ॥ २.१.३

etasmājjāyate prāṇo manaḥ sarvendriyāṇi ca |

khaṃ vāyurjyotirāpaḥ pṛthivī viśvasya dhāriṇī || 2.1.3

एतस्मात् जायते प्राणः मनः सर्वेन्द्रियाणि च ।

खं वायुः ज्योतिः आपः पृथिवी विश्वस्य धारिणी ॥

एतस्मात्[m5/1] From This प्राणः[m1/1] the life force मनः[n1/1] intellect सर्वेन्द्रियाणि[n1/3] all senses च[0] and, खं[n1/1] space वायुः[m1/1] air ज्योतिः[n1/1] light आपः[f1/3] water विश्वस्य[m6/1] for all beings धारिणी[f1/1] the support पृथिवी[f1/1] the planet earth जायते[iii/1] लट् takes birth ॥

2.1.3 From the majestic effulgent Being,

the conscious life force,
the reasoning faculty,
all senses and organs,
the vast empty spaces so essential for growth,
the nourishing air,
the light and fire,
the water and fluids, and
the divine mother Earth that contains and sustains
all beings and things

is manufactured.

अग्निर्मूर्धा चक्षुषी चन्द्रसूर्यौ दिशः श्रोत्रे वाग् विवृताश्च वेदाः ।
वायुः प्राणो हृदयं विश्वमस्य पद्भ्यां पृथिवी ह्येष सर्वभूतान्तरात्मा ॥ ४

agnirmūrdhā cakṣuṣī candrasūryau diśaḥ śrotre vāg
vivṛtāśca vedāḥ | vāyuḥ prāṇo hṛdayaṃ viśvamasya
padbhyāṃ pṛthivī hyeṣa sarvabhūtāntarātmā || 2.1.4

अग्निः मूर्धा चक्षुषी चन्द्रसूर्यौ दिशः श्रोत्रे वाक् विवृताः च वेदाः ।
वायुः प्राणः हृदयं विश्वम् अस्य पद्भ्यां पृथिवी हि एषः सर्वभूत–
अन्तरात्मा ॥

अस्य $^{n6/1}$ His

मूर्धा $^{m1/1}$ अग्निः $^{m1/1}$ forehead is like the brilliant fire,

चक्षुषी $^{n1/2}$ चन्द्रसूर्यौ $^{m1/2}$ eyes are like the sun & moon,

श्रोत्रे $^{n1/2}$ दिशः $^{m1/1}$ ears are like the four quarters,

वाक् $^{f1/1}$ विवृताः $^{PPP\,m1/3}$ वेदाः $^{m1/3}$ speech is like the

emanated scriptures, च ^{0} and (his)

प्राणः $^{m1/1}$ वायुः $^{m1/1}$ life-force is all pervading air ,

हृदयं $^{n1/1}$ विश्वम् $^{n1/1}$ heart is the pulsating universe,

पद्भ्यां $^{m5/2}$ पृथिवी $^{f1/1}$ earth – to move forward,

एषः $^{m1/1}$ हि ^{0} सर्वभूत–अन्तरात्मा $^{m1/1}$ ॥ Verily it is the
innermost soul of all beings and things.

2.1.4 And of the Divine we can visualize

- fire as the forehead for crystal clear thinking
- moon and sun as the eyes that see in night as well as day, the eyes that observe everything since they do not shut nor rest
- the four quarters as the ears that hear every little tremor, shake, and pin drop
- diverse scriptures, textbooks, and methods of schooling and instruction as speech
- interstellar space and air as the throbbing life-force,
- the universe with ceaseless activity as its pulsating heart
- this planet Earth its domain of target setting and goal attaining – a step forward.

The Brahman is the innermost soul of every being. He is contained in the sinner and the saint. He is in the flower and the paint.

तस्मादग्निः समिधो यस्य सूर्यः सोमात् पर्जन्य ओषधयः पृथिव्याम् ।
पुमान् रेतः सिञ्चति योषितायां बह्वीः प्रजाः पुरुषात् सम्प्रसूताः ॥२.१.५
tasmādagniḥ samidho yasya sūryaḥ somāt parjanya
oṣadhayaḥ pṛthivyām | pumān retaḥ siñcati yoṣitāyāṃ
bahvīḥ prajāḥ puruṣāt samprasūtāḥ ∥ 2.1.5

तस्मात् अग्निः समिधः यस्य सूर्यः सोमात् पर्जन्यः ओषधयः पृथिव्याम्
। पुमान् रेतः सिञ्चति योषितायां बह्वीः प्रजाः पुरुषात् सम्प्रसूताः ॥

तस्मात् ^m5/1 From Him

अग्निः ^m1/1 fire समिधः ^m1/1 the catalyst यस्य ^m6/1 just as
सूर्यः ^m1/1 the sun,

पृथिव्याम् ^f7/1 on earth सोमात् ^m5/1 from the moon पर्जन्यः
^m1/1 rain cloud ओषधयः ^f1/3 herbs ।

योषितायां ^f7/1 in the female पुमान् ^m1/1 the male member

रेतः ^n2/1 seminal fluid सिञ्चति ^iii/1 लट् injects,

बह्वीः ^f2/3 so many प्रजाः ^m1/3 plants and living beings

पुरुषात् ^m5/1 from the supreme godhead सम्प्रसूताः ^PPP m1/3

॥ arose

2.1.5 The cycle of procreation proceeds from

- Fire that ignites passion and like the Sun makes fusion possible
- Clouds that bring rain and cause food to grow
- Moon that infuses vitality into herbs in the soil
- The Male who is thus well nourished by the food becomes empowered to make the female pregnant.

Many such occasions cause multiple births to happen. All types of flora, fauna and beings are thus created.

तस्मादु ऋचः साम यजूंषि दीक्षा यज्ञाश्च सर्वे क्रतवो दक्षिणाश्च ।
संवत्सरश्च यजमानश्च लोकाः सोमो यत्र पवते यत्र सूर्यः ॥ २.१.६

tasmād ṛcaḥ sāma yajūṃṣi dīkṣā yajñāśca sarve kratavo
dakṣiṇāśca | saṃvatsaraśca yajamānaśca lokāḥ somo yatra
pavate yatra sūryaḥ ॥ 2.1.6

तस्मात् ऋचः साम यजूंषि दीक्षा यज्ञाः च सर्वे क्रतवः दक्षिणाः च ।
संवत्सरः च यजमानः च लोकाः सोमः यत्र पवते यत्र सूर्यः ॥

तस्मात् $^{m5/1}$ From Him

ऋचः $^{f1/1}$ cosmic energyसाम $^{n1/1}$ harmonizing energy

यजूंषि $^{n1/3}$ individual thought currents दीक्षा $^{f1/1}$ skill

imparting च ^{0} and ,

सर्वे $^{m1/3}$ all types यज्ञाः $^{m1/3}$ manufacturing processes च ^{0}

and क्रतवः $^{m1/3}$ works for sustenance दक्षिणाः $^{f1/3}$

earnings ।

संवत्सरः $^{m1/1}$ the yearly cycle of time च ^{0} and,

यजमानः $^{m1/1}$ the manager च ^{0} and,

लोकाः $^{m1/3}$ the galaxies यत्र ^{0} where सोमः $^{m1/1}$ the moon

पवते $^{iii/1}$ लट् blesses, यत्र ^{0} where सूर्यः $^{m1/1}$ the sun ॥

2.1.6 From Brahman emerge the energies - Rik that manifests cosmic laws, Sama that balances, Yajus that formulates individual emotions and thought processes.

From Brahman emerges the special faculty of training, imparting skill, and education, especially from parents to children for all mammals.

From Brahman the systems of manufacturing and gainful employment. Thereby the merits and earnings.

Due to Brahman the yearly cycle of time comes into existence.

Due to Brahman some assume authority and status and can thus govern and conduct affairs.

Due to Brahman the galaxies got formed.

And to Brahman's credit the all fulfilling, purifying, and blessing nature of the moon and the sun that shine on all.

तस्माच्च देवा बहुधा सम्प्रसूताः साध्या मनुष्याः पशवो वयांसि ।
प्राणापानौ व्रीहियवौ तपश्च श्रद्धा सत्यं ब्रह्मचर्यं विधिश्च ॥ २.१.७
tasmācca devā bahudhā samprasūtāḥ sādhyā manuṣyāḥ
paśavo vayāṃsi | prāṇāpānau vrīhiyavau tapaśca śraddha
satyaṃ brahmacaryaṃ vidhiśca ॥ 2.1.7

तस्मात् च देवाः बहुधा सम्प्रसूताः साध्याः मनुष्याः पशवः वयांसि ।
प्राणापानौ व्रीहियवौ तपः च श्रद्धा सत्यं ब्रह्मचर्यं विधिः च ॥

तस्मात् $^{m5/1}$ From Him

बहुधा ^{0} of differing strengths and skills देवाः $^{m1/3}$ the

celestial beings सम्प्रसूताः $^{PPP\ m1/3}$ were created च ^{0} and

साध्याः $^{m1/3}$ perfected beings मनुष्याः $^{m1/3}$ mankind पशवः

$^{m1/3}$ animal kingdom वयांसि $^{m1/3}$ flying creatures । च ^{0}

and प्राणापानौ $^{m1/2}$ the prana and apana vital airs व्रीहियवौ

$^{m1/2}$ the rice and barley grains च ^{0} and

तपः $^{m1/1}$ value system श्रद्धा $^{f1/1}$ devotion सत्यं $^{n1/1}$

truthfulness ब्रह्मचर्यं $^{n1/1}$ practical and safe use of items

and conservative habits विधिः $^{m1/1}$ procedure of any

type ॥

2.1.7 Due to Brahman's will manifested gods with varying talents, the enlightened masters, the common folks, animals and birds.

Brahman willed the involuntary functions like respiration and excretion.

Brahman then created all grains and delicacies.

Brahman advocated the spiritual practices of rigorous discipline, staunch faith, truthfulness, balance in action and inaction, and social laws.

सप्त प्राणाः प्रभवन्ति तस्मात् सप्तार्चिषः समिधः सप्त होमाः ।
सप्त इमे लोका येषु चरन्ति प्राणा गुहाशया निहिताः सप्त सप्त ॥ २.१.८

sapta prāṇāḥ prabhavanti tasmāt saptārciṣaḥ samidhaḥ
sapta homāḥ | sapta ime lokā yeṣu caranti prāṇā guhāśayā
nihitāḥ sapta sapta || 2.1.8

सप्त प्राणाः प्रभवन्ति तस्मात् सप्त अर्चिषः समिधः सप्त होमाः ।
सप्त इमे लोकाः येषु चरन्ति प्राणाः गुहाशायाः निहिताः सप्त सप्त ॥

तस्मात् [m5/1] From Him सप्त [mfn1/3] seven प्राणाः [m1/3]
pranayama प्रभवन्ति [iii/3 लट्] are major,
सप्त [m1/3] अर्चिषः [m1/1] flames समिधः [m1/1] services सप्त [m1/3]
होमाः [m1/3] earning activities |
इमे [m1/3] these सप्त [m1/3] लोकाः [m1/3] planets येषु [m7/3]
wherein सप्त [m1/3] प्राणाः [m1/3] energies चरन्ति [miii/3 लट्]
circulate
गुहाशायाः [m1/3] deep in the caverns निहिताः [PPP m1/3] seated
सप्त [m1/3] ||

70

2.1.8 Seven is his magical figure. He made

- प्राणाः 7 pranayama – nadi shodhana, ujjayi, bhastrika, kapalbhati, bhramari, agnisara, sudarshan kriya
- अर्चिषः 7 light colors –vibgyor - rainbow
- समिधः 7 service acts needed by every household – cooking, cleaning, washing, gardening, carpentry, plumbing, electricals
- होमाः 7 types of earning activity - farming, mining, manufacturing, processing, trading, publishing, counseling
- लोकाः 7 continents/seas/planets
- प्राणाः 7 chakras, the major energy centers - mooladhara to sahasrara

7 deep seated virtues are his signature or presence.

See Patanjali Yoga Sutras – a) Friendship, b) Kindness, c) Cheerfulness, d) Absence of fear, e) Absence of obsession, f) Clarity of mind, and g) Pragmatic vision.

अतः समुद्रा गिरयश्च सर्वेऽस्मात् स्यन्दन्ते सिन्धवः सर्वरूपाः ।
अतश्च सर्वा ओषधयो रसश्च येनैष भूतैस्तिष्ठते ह्यन्तरात्मा ॥ २.१.९

atah samudrā girayaśca sarve'smāt syandante sindhavah
sarvarūpāh | ataśca sarvā oṣadhayo rasaśca yenaiṣa
bhūtaistiṣṭhate hyantarātmā ॥ 2.1.9

अतः समुद्राः गिरयः च सर्वे अस्मात् स्यन्दन्ते सिन्धवः सर्वरूपाः ।
अतः च सर्वाः ओषधयः रसः च येन एषः भूतैः तिष्ठते हि अन्तरात्मा
॥

अतः ^{0} So also

सर्वे $^{m1/3}$ all समुद्राः $^{m1/3}$ oceans गिरयः $^{m1/3}$ hills च ^{0} and,
अस्मात् $^{m5/1}$ From it
सर्वरूपाः $^{m1/3}$ all kinds सिन्धवः $^{m1/3}$ rivers स्यन्दन्ते $^{iii/3}$ लट्
trickle and flow ।
अतः ^{0} च ^{0} and also
सर्वाः $^{f1/3}$ all types ओषधयः $^{f1/3}$ plants and herbs रसः $^{m1/1}$
sap, juices and pleasurable delights च ^{0} and,
येन $^{m3/1}$ by which हि ^{0} verily एषः $^{m1/1}$ this भूतैः $^{m3/3}$ by the
bodies अन्तरात्मा $^{m1/1}$ soul तिष्ठते $^{iii/1}$ लट् resides

2.1.9 So also from him the calm oceans and majestic mountains manifest. And water bodies of varied hue, blue lakes, gurgling streams, roaring rivers.

By his will nutritious vegetables and juicy fruits, all sensuous pleasures.

And in the midst of all this splendid distraction, he ensconces himself, placid-pure-innocent.

पुरुष एवेदं विश्वं कर्म तपो ब्रह्म परामृतम् ।
एतद्यो वेद निहितं गुहायां सोऽविद्याग्रन्थि विकिरतीह सोम्य ॥ २.१.१०

puruṣa evedaṃ viśvaṃ karma tapo brahma parāmṛtam |
etadyo veda nihitaṃ guhāyāṃ so'vidyāgranthiṃ vikiratīha
somya || 2.1.10

पुरुषः एव इदं विश्वं कर्म तपः ब्रह्म परामृतम् ।
एतत् यः वेद निहितं गुहायां सः अविद्याग्रन्थि विकिरति इह सोम्य ॥

इदं $^{n1/1}$ this पुरुषः $^{m1/1}$ supreme being एव ^{0} alone विश्वं $^{n1/1}$
the universe परामृतम् $^{n1/1}$ the sweetest nectar कर्म $^{n1/1}$
the activity तपः $^{m1/1}$ the austerity ब्रह्म $^{n1/1}$ the Infinity |

गुहायां $^{f7/1}$ deep within निहितं $^{PPP\,n1/1}$ well assimilated
एतत् $^{n1/1}$ this यः $^{m1/1}$ who वेद $^{iii/1}$ लट् recognizes,
सः $^{m1/1}$ he इह ^{0} in this life itself अविद्याग्रन्थि $^{m2/1}$ the
messy conflict विकिरति $^{iii/1}$ लट् shears apart
सोम्य $^{Vm1/1}$ O sincere child ||

2.1.10 Both flavors, The paths of Karma Yoga and
of Gyana Yoga, find his favor and his complete
approval.

The soul that glimpses this truth, lives life with such
clarity of vision in total acceptance, that soul
triumphs, sheds the knotty fricative ignorance in this
life itself, and attains Nirvana.

O beloved seeker! Own this teaching and you also
become immortal.

Here ends the first term of the second year on a
promising note.

2nd Year 2nd Semester

आविः सन्निहितं गुहाचरन्नाम महत् पदमत्रैतत् समर्पितम् ।
एजत् प्राणन्निमिषच्च यदेतज्जानथ सदसद्वरेण्यं परं विज्ञानाद्यद्वरिष्ठं
प्रजानाम् ॥ २.२.१

āviḥ sannihitaṃ guhācarannāma mahat padamatraitat
samarpitam | ejat prāṇannimiṣacca yadetajjānatha
sadasadvareṇyaṃ paraṃ vijñānād yad variṣṭhaṃ
prajānām || 2.2.1

आविः सन्निहितं गुहाचरत् नाम महत् पदम् अत्र एतत् समर्पितम् ।
एजत् प्राणत् निमिषत् च यत् एतत् जानथ सत् असत् वरेण्यं परं
विज्ञानात् यत् वरिष्ठं प्रजानाम् ॥

नाम $^{n1/1}$ the name आविः $^{m1/1}$ luminous सन्निहितं $^{PPP\,n1/1}$
firmly fixed पदम् $^{n1/1}$ foundation गुहाचरत् $^{PrPA\,n1/1}$ fluidly
circulating in the heart cavity
अत्र ^{0} herein एतत् $^{n1/1}$ this महत् $^{n1/1}$ big universe समर्पितम्
$^{PPP\,n1/1}$ centered |
यत् $^{n1/1}$ that एजत् $^{PrPA\,n1/1\,शतृ}$ moves प्राणत् $^{PrPA\,n1/1\,शतृ}$
breathes निमिषत् $^{PrPA\,n1/1\,शतृ}$ winks च ^{0} and एतत् $^{n1/1}$ this
सत् $^{n1/1}$ real असत् $^{n1/1}$ imaginary परं $^{n1/1}$ विज्ञानात् $^{n5/1}$
beyond logic , यत् $^{n1/1}$ that वरिष्ठं $^{n1/1}$ ultimate वरेण्यं $^{n1/1}$
wish प्रजानाम् $^{n6/3}$ of all beings जानथ you all recognize ||

जानथ Vedic usage for जानीथ $^{ii/3}$ लट् in the sense of विधि लिङ्

$2.2.1$ It is effulgent अविः, near at hand and ready to help सन्निहितं, giving many glimpses and nudges, but packaged in
the ordinary easy to miss moments.

So a silent stable mind is required to sense it moving in a heart that is filled with love. A breath that is quiver free makes it possible.

The supreme prize is he, he is the one worth seeking. He is the fountain of joy and one's firm foundation.

गुहाचरं नाम यत् महत् पदम्
He is both the dance and the dance floor for whatever that moves, breathes, or blinks.
अत्र एजत् प्राणत् निमिषत् च एतत् सर्वं समर्पितम्
Grasp this essential truth with an open mind.
एतत् जानथ
He is All that is eternal and also all that is transient.
यत् सत् असत्
He is all that is desirable, attractive and luxurious.
वरेण्यम्
He is top-seeded, topmost, the VVIP.वरिष्ठं

And he is too big to be cognized by the mind, imagined by the heart, or contained in any brainwave. तथा प्रजानां विज्ञानात् परम् ॥

यदर्चिमद्यदणुभ्योऽणु च यस्मिंल्लोका निहिता लोकिनश्च ।
तदेतदक्षरं ब्रह्म स प्राणस्तदु वाङ् मनः । तदेतत् सत्यं तदमृतं तद्
वेद्धव्यं सोम्य विद्धि ॥ २.२.२

yadarcimadyadaṇubhyo'ṇu ca yasmiṁllokā nihitā lokinaśca | tadetadakṣaraṃ brahma sa prāṇastadu vāṅ manaḥ | tadetat satyaṃ tadamṛtaṃ tad veddhavyaṃ somya viddhi || 2.2.2

यत् अर्चिमत् यत् अणुभ्यः अणु च यस्मिन् लोकाः निहिताः लोकिनः च । तत् एतत् अक्षरं ब्रह्म सः प्राणः तत् उ वाक् मनः । तत् एतत् सत्यं तत् अमृतं तत् वेद्धव्यं सोम्य विद्धि ॥

यत् $^{n1/1}$ that अर्चिमत् $^{n1/1}$ effulgent यत् $^{n1/1}$ that अणुभ्यः $^{n5/3}$ amongst all atomic things अणु $^{n1/1}$ minute च ^{0} and यस्मिन् $^{n7/1}$ in which लोकाः $^{m1/3}$ the lands लोकिनः च ^{0} and $^{m1/3}$ the beings निहिताः $^{PPP\,m1/3}$ contained |

तत् $^{n1/1}$ that एतत् $^{n1/1}$ this अक्षरं $^{n1/1}$ inviolable ब्रह्म $^{n1/1}$ Infinity
सः $^{m1/1}$ He प्राणः $^{m1/1}$ the life force, तत् $^{n1/1}$ that उ ^{0} verily वाक् $^{f1/1}$ the speech मनः $^{n1/1}$ the intellect |
तत् $^{n1/1}$ that एतत् $^{n1/1}$ this अमृतं $^{n1/1}$ precious सत्यं $^{n1/1}$ fact, सोम्य $^{Vm1/1}$ O earnest seeker तत् $^{n1/1}$ that वेद्धव्यं $^{n1/1}$ worthy of aim तत् $^{n1/1}$ that विद्धि $^{iii/1\,लोट्}$ thee may aim ||

2.2.2 That which glows brilliantly and is hence visible to all यत् अर्चिमत्

That which is subtler than the finest particle and hence can escape being noticed by the best of scientists यत् अणुभ्यः अपि अणु च

That in which all galaxies and black holes are contained यस्मिन् लोकाः

That in which all thoughts, fantasies, emotions and sensations, desires, expectations and aspirations are clearly experienced लोकिनः च निहिताः

That is This तत् एतत्

Named the immutable Brahman अक्षरं ब्रह्म

He is the life story of all beings सः प्राणः

It is the sound emerging from every lip तत् उ वाक्

It is the cause of every reason or decision मनः

That is the Truth तत् एतत् सत्यम्

That is the sweetest delight. तत् अमृतम्

By the full force of the mind and all faculties, Seek, Respect, Understand and Assimilate तत् मनसा वेद्धव्यं

O Worthy Aspirant! That Brahman you must get schooled in. Make that your Priority, Focus, Goal.

धनुर्गृहीत्वौपनिषदं महास्त्रं शरं ह्युपासानिशितं सन्धयीत ।
आयम्य तद् भावगतेन चेतसा लक्ष्यं तदेवाऽक्षरं सोम्य विद्धि ॥ २.२.३

dhanurgrhītvaupaniṣadaṃ mahāstraṃ śaraṃ
hyupāsāniśitaṃ sandhayīta | āyamya tad bhāvagatena
cetasā lakṣyaṃ tadevākṣaraṃ somya viddhi || 2.2.3

धनुः गृहीत्वा औपनिषदं महास्त्रं शरं हि उपासा निशितं सन्धयीत ।
आयम्य तद्–भावगतेन चेतसा लक्ष्यं तत् एव अक्षरं सोम्य विद्धि ॥

धनुः $^{m1/1}$ the bow हि ^{0} verily गृहीत्वा ^{gerund} having strung
महास्त्रं $^{n2/1}$ the principal thought arrow औपनिषदं $^{n2/1}$
infused with wisdom, शरं $^{m2/1}$ the arrow निशितं $^{PPP\ n1/1}$
sharpened उपासा $^{n3/1}$ by regular meditation सन्धयीत $^{ii/3}$
विधि लिङ् you all must beautifully aim ।
सोम्य $^{Vm1/1}$ O noble son! आयम्य $^{0\ ल्यप्}$ having drawn
तद्भावगतेन $^{m3/1\ क}$ with total concentration चेतसा $^{n3/1}$ by
the mind तत् $^{n1/1}$ that अक्षरं $^{n1/1}$ pure लक्ष्यं $^{n1/1}$ aim एव ^{0}
alone विद्धि $^{iii/1\ लोट्}$ thee may pierce ॥

2.2.3 By the practice of Upanishad, sitting close, available, all ears,

String your bow of deep adoration, honor and reverence.

Fix on it the arrow of your senses with laser like sharpness, your mind immersed in meditative contemplation, your body thoroughly loose and relaxed.

Thus taking aim at the clear target that shows itself in the tranquil heart, loosen your arrow within, enter that Divine space with good cheer.

Become one and United with that.

Fuse, melt, dissolve, lose yourself in that infinite peace.

Now the means of practice, the steps of Sadhana

प्रणवो धनुः शरो ह्यात्मा ब्रह्म तल्लक्ष्यमुच्यते ।
अप्रमत्तेन वेद्धव्यं शरवत् तन्मयो भवेत् ॥ २.२.४

praṇavo dhanuḥ śaro hyātmā brahma tallakṣyamucyate |
apramattena veddhavyaṃ śaravat tanmayo bhavet || 2.2.4

प्रणवः धनुः शरः हि आत्मा ब्रह्म तत् लक्ष्यम् उच्यते ।
अप्रमत्तेन वेद्धव्यं शरवत् तन्मयः भवेत् ॥

प्रणवः $^{m1/1}$ sacred syllable Om हि ^{0} verily धनुः $^{m1/1}$ bow, शरः $^{m1/1}$ arrow आत्मा $^{m1/1}$ soul, ब्रह्म $^{n1/1}$ Brahman तत् $^{n1/1}$ that लक्ष्यम् $^{n2/1}$ goal उच्यते $^{iii/1}$ लट् कर्मणि is taught । अप्रमत्तेन $^{m3/1}$ with decisiveness वेद्धव्यं $^{n1/1}$ should be hit शरवत् ^{0} as the arrow becomes one after hitting the target तन्मयः $^{m1/1}$ absorbed भवेत् $^{iii/1}$ विधि लिङ् you should be ॥

2.2.4 The chant of Om

 forms a great sound envelope that equips the mind with resourcefulness, as the twang of a great bow heralds victory.

The Soul united with the body, the senses, the intellect, the citta and the ego becomes a yogic arrow that speeds unerringly towards its aim.

The target is only that one God, also known as Brahman, Shiva, Tao and by other diverse names.

or

You may call it Love, Kindness, Purity.

Use your entire will, attention, intention, and sincere earnestness to attain the Lord and merge with him.

Let Brahman be your prime passion and ultimate reward. Make all your activities resound with his name, also called Om.

Certainly this birth is precious and in this very body justify it by living a yogic life and attain Oneness with the Supreme.

यस्मिन् द्यौः पृथिवी चान्तरिक्षमोतं मनः सह प्राणैश्च सर्वैः ।
तमेवैकं जानथ आत्मानमन्या वाचो विमुञ्चथामृतस्यैष सेतुः ॥ २.२.५

yasmin dyauḥ pṛthivī cāntarikṣamotaṃ manaḥ saha
prāṇaiśca sarvaiḥ | tamevaikaṃ jānatha ātmānamanyā
vāco vimuñcathāmṛtasyaiṣa setuḥ ॥ 2.2.5

यस्मिन् द्यौः पृथिवी च अन्तरिक्षम् ओतं मनः सह प्राणैः च सर्वैः ।
तम् एव एकं जानथ आत्मानम् अन्याः वाचः विमुञ्चथ अमृतस्य एषः
सेतुः ॥

यस्मिन् [m7/1] in what द्यौः [m1/1] heaven च [0] and पृथिवी [f1/1] earth, अन्तरिक्षम् [n1/1] intervening space च [0] and मनः [n1/1] mind सह [0] with सर्वैः [m3/3] with all प्राणैः [m3/3] with vital airs ओतं [PPP n1/1] immersed ।
तम् [m2/1] that एकं [m2/1] one आत्मानम् [m2/1] soul एव [0] alone जानथ [ii/3] you all should study,
अन्याः [f5/1] from other extraneous वाचः [f1/3] talks and discussions विमुञ्चथ [ii/3] लट् you be wary,
अमृतस्य [m6/1] of the divine एषः [m1/1] this सेतुः [m1/1] the bridge ॥

विमुञ्चथ in the sense of विमुञ्चत [ii/3] लोट्

2.2.5 Another thing that shall greatly help your Sadhana is to mind your tongue from uttering anything casual, frivolous, grumbling or hurtful.

Stop loose talk forthwith.

Refrain from hurting anyone through your tongue.

Then instantly you shall realize that all that you see –
- bodies, objects, flora and fauna; and
- all that you interact with - land, space, and atmosphere; and also
- all that you experience within - breath, mind, heart, and the rest

It is all tightly interwoven in the Brahman, nay it is all composed of Brahman alone.

The moment you get such a glimpse; know that you are well on track, your aim is soon achieved, Nirvana awaits you.

अरा इव रथनाभौ संहता यत्र नाड्यः स एषोऽन्तश्चरते बहुधा जायमानः
ॐ इत्येवं ध्यायथ आत्मानं स्वस्ति वः पाराय तमसः परस्तात् ॥ ६
arā iva rathanābhau saṃhatā yatra nāḍyaḥ sa
eṣo'ntaścarate bahudhā jāyamānaḥ |
oṃ ityevaṃ dhyāyatha ātmānaṃ svasti vaḥ pārāya
tamasaḥ parastāt || 2.2.6

अराः इव रथनाभौ संहताः यत्र नाड्यः सः एषः अन्तः चरते बहुधा
जायमानः । ॐ इति एवं ध्यायथ आत्मानं स्वस्ति वः पाराय तमसः
परस्तात् ॥

यत्र ^{0} where नाड्यः $^{f1/3}$ nerve channels इव ^{0} just as अराः $^{m1/3}$ spokes रथनाभौ $^{m2/1}$ nave of a wheel संहताः $^{PPP\ f1/3}$ meet
सः $^{m1/1}$ he अन्तः ^{0} within एषः $^{m1/1}$ this बहुधा ^{0} diversely जायमानः $^{PrPA\ m1/1}$ शानच् multiplying चरते $^{iii/1}$ लट् moves |
ॐ^0 "Om" इति ^{0} thus एवं ^{0} alone आत्मानं $^{m2/1}$ on the inner divine ध्यायथ $^{ii/3}$ लट् contemplate,
पाराय $^{n4/1}$ for going beyond तमसः $^{n1/1}$ suffering स्वस्ति ^{0} Blessings, वः $^{mfn2/3}$ you all परस्तात् ^{0} rise above ॥

2.2.6 Your navel center is the hub on which all nerves connect like the spokes on the wheel of life.

Deep inside your heart is the space where Brahman resides and rules your world by twitching the nerves, throttling some, loosening others.

Everywhere it is the same, each particle, ant, virus or human, is so impregnated and ruled by Brahman.

And particularly in this human body - sense him, identify with the inner conscience, and befriend him by means of the sacred syllable Om.

Meditate on Brahman by chanting Om.

That shall surely make the task of crossing the dangerous river of inky darkness unscathed.

You shall certainly pass from this world guilt free, blame free, Free.

Gurudev advises to suffix Om with a mahavakya e.g.
Om Namah Shivaya,
Om Namo Bhagavate Vasudevaya
Om Tat Sat, etc.

यः सर्वज्ञः सर्वविद् यस्यैष महिमा भुवि । दिव्ये ब्रह्मपुरे ह्येष
व्योम्न्यात्मा प्रतिष्ठितः । मनोमयः प्राणशरीरनेता प्रतिष्ठितोऽन्ने हृदयं
सन्निधाय । तदु विज्ञानेन परिपश्यन्ति धीरा आनन्दरूपममृतं यदु
विभाति ॥ २.२.७

yaḥ sarvajñaḥ sarvavid yasyaiṣa mahimā bhuvi | divye
brahmapure hyeṣa vyomnyātmā pratiṣṭhitaḥ |
manomayaḥ prāṇaśarīranetā pratiṣṭhito'nne hṛdayaṃ
sannidhāya | tad vijñānena paripaśyanti dhīrā
ānandarūpamamṛtaṃ yad vibhāti ॥ 2.2.7

यः सर्वज्ञः सर्ववित् यस्य एषः महिमा भुवि । दिव्ये ब्रह्मपुरे हि एषः
व्योम्नि आत्मा प्रतिष्ठितः । मनोमयः प्राण-शरीर-नेता प्रतिष्ठितः अन्ने
हृदयं सन्निधाय । तत् विज्ञानेन परिपश्यन्ति धीराः आनन्दरूपम्
अमृतं यत् विभाति ॥

यः^{m1/1} who सर्वज्ञः^{m1/1} all knowledgeable सर्ववित्^{n1/1} all perceiving यस्य^{m6/1} whose एषः^{m1/1} this महिमा^{m1/1} glory भुवि^{f7/1} on earth । दिव्ये^{n7/1} in the luminous ब्रह्मपुरे^{n7/1} in the township of infinity हि⁰ verily एषः^{m1/1} this व्योम्नि^{m7/1} in space आत्मा^{m1/1} soul प्रतिष्ठितः^{PPP m1/1} comfortably seated । मनोमयः^{m1/1} one conditioned by thoughts प्राणशरीरनेता^{m1/1} owner of life-force and body प्रतिष्ठितः^{PPP m1/1} firmly placed अन्ने^{n7/1} in the food हृदयं^{n1/1} heart सन्निधाय^{0 ल्यप्} close vicinity । तत्^{n1/1} it विज्ञानेन^{n3/1} by scientific vision परिपश्यन्ति^{iii/3 लट्} fully realize धीराः^{m1/3} the brave आनन्दरूपम्^{n1/1} joyful nature अमृतं^{n1/1} strengthening nectar यत्^{n1/1} which विभाति^{iii/1 लट्} illumines ॥

2.2.7 The great men and women make life worth living by setting an example. Their life has all the flavors and pitfalls that come to you as well, yet they live with a graceful charm.

The Brahman is awakened in them, or we can say Brahman owns their body, Brahman rules their mind, Brahman guides them in all transactions, and Brahman is all they care for.

They are discriminating and particular about their habits, food, lifestyle and sangat. They are careful whose company they choose and whom they avoid.

This helps them sail smoothly in life. This sets them apart from the rest. This gets them the epithet - the bold, the beautiful, the successful brave.

If you ask them - have you seen God? Their reply is almost always –
- God is the only light my eyes see,
- God alone is he who comes to mind,
- God colors my thoughts, and
- God rules my emotions.

भिद्यते हृदयग्रन्थिश्छिद्यन्ते सर्वसंशायाः ।
क्षीयन्ते चास्य कर्माणि तस्मिन् दृष्टे परावरे ॥ २.२.८

bhidyate hṛdayagranthiśchidyante sarvasaṃśayāḥ |
kṣīyante cāsya karmāṇi tasmin dṛṣṭe parāvare || 2.2.8

भिद्यते हृदयग्रन्थिः छिद्यन्ते सर्वसंशायाः ।
क्षीयन्ते च अस्य कर्माणि तस्मिन् दृष्टे परावरे ॥

हृदयग्रन्थिः $^{m1/1}$ conflict in the heart, undigested thought भिद्यते $^{iii/1}$ लट् कर्मणि resolves, सर्वसंशायाः $^{m1/3}$ all suspicions and doubts छिद्यन्ते $^{iii/3}$ लट् clears |

अस्य $^{m6/1}$ of him च ^{0} and कर्माणि $^{n1/3}$ impressions and bias क्षीयन्ते $^{iii/3}$ लट् weakens,

तस्मिन् $^{n7/1}$ in those दृष्टे $^{PPP\ n7/1}$ in perception परावरे $^{n7/1}$ in opposite values ॥

2.2.8 Pure becomes the heart in their company.
Doubts vanish, guilt melts, impressions and karma
get burnt.

Such is the blazing company of the wise. That is what
an enlightened master does.

The Guru resolves all conflicts, cures all ills, he brings
you home to Oneness.

This happens in those who are able to see that
Opposite values are complementary in nature.

Those who can sense the Divine's hand in ups and
downs, in fluctuating seasons, joys and frustrations.

Who never ever lay the blame on anyone, who do not
nourish guilt, nor harbor doubt.

हिरण्मये परे कोशो विरजं ब्रह्म निष्कलम् ।
तच्छुभ्रं ज्योतिषां ज्योतिस्तद् यदात्मविदो विदुः ॥ २.२.९

hiraṇmaye pare kośe virajaṃ brahma niṣkalam |
tacchubhraṃ jyotiṣāṃ jyotistad yadātmavido viduḥ ॥ 2.2.9

हिरण्मये परे कोशो विरजं ब्रह्म निष्कलम् ।
तत् शुभ्रं ज्योतिषां ज्योतिः तत् यत् आत्मविदः विदुः ॥

हिरण्मये $^{m7/1}$ in the golden परे $^{n7/1}$ in the very difficult to reach कोशो $^{m7/1}$ in the space निष्कलम् $^{n1/1}$ the undivided ब्रह्म $^{n1/1}$ Infinity विरजं $^{PPP\,n1/1}$ shone unstained ।
तत् $^{n1/1}$ it शुभ्रं $^{n1/1}$ the auspicious ज्योतिषां $^{m6/3}$ of all lights ज्योतिः $^{m1/1}$ the brilliance,
तत् $^{n1/1}$ that यत् $^{n1/1}$ which आत्मविदः $^{m1/3}$ knowers of Brahman विदुः $^{i/3}$ लट् know ॥

2.2.9 You become golden. You become luminous. You sparkle and shine, your light reaches far and wide.

Your purity speaks for itself, your divinity is your ticket.

You are hailed as a knower of Brahman. You become a realized soul.

The Brahman is eulogized. The Saint is praised.

It is very hard to attain sainthood. It is most difficult to become pure. It needs lots of patient practice to achieve a level where you become the lighthouse to guide many on the path.

This can only be appreciated by those at the top. Those who made it through.

Only an able mother knows how much effort is needed to raise good children. Only the housewife knows how much time and energy is required to cook something lip-smacking delicious and nutritious to boot!

न तत्र सूर्यो भाति न चन्द्रतारकं नेमा विद्युतो भान्ति कुतोऽयमग्निः ।
तमेव भान्तमनुभाति सर्वं तस्य भासा सर्वमिदं विभाति ॥ २.२.१०

<u>A famous and oft quoted verse from the Upanishads.</u>

na tatra sūryo bhāti na candratārakaṃ nemā vidyuto
bhānti kuto'yamagniḥ | tameva bhāntamanubhāti sarvaṃ
tasya bhāsā sarvamidaṃ vibhāti || 2.2.10

न तत्र सूर्यः भाति न चन्द्रतारकं न इमाः विद्युतः भान्ति कुतः अयम्
अग्निः । तम् एव भान्तम् अनुभाति सर्वं तस्य भासा सर्वम् इदं विभाति
॥

तत्र ^{0} there सूर्यः $^{m1/1}$ sunlight न ^{0} not भाति $^{iii/1}$ illumines ,
न ^{0} not चन्द्रतारकं $^{n1/1}$ moonlight or starlight,
इमाः $^{f1/3}$ these विद्युतः $^{f1/3}$ lightning flashes न ^{0} do not
भान्ति $^{iii/3}$ लट् reveal,
कुतः ^{0} how then अयम् $^{m1/1}$ this अग्निः $^{m1/1}$ flame ।
तम् $^{m2/1}$ that एव ^{0} alone भान्तम् $^{PrPA\ n1/1}$ शतृ is shining,
भासा $^{f3/1}$ by its light सर्व $^{n1/1}$ all इदं $^{n1/1}$ this अनुभाति $^{iii/1}$ लट्
reflects, सर्वम् $^{n1/1}$ all तस्य $^{n6/1}$ of this विभाति $^{iii/1}$ लट्
illumines

2.2.10 There no sensory light reaches, that is fathomless, silent and still.

There is no distinction there, no features of any sort even when examined under the blazing sun or the cool moonlight or even the faintest star. Purity is a seamless whole, that the light of intellect does not grasp, nor does lightening illumine.

Then how could our small candle flames or fancy torches or puny ego reach there?

By Brahman is the functioning of men and machines, By it is governed the tempest and the breeze.

All is made brilliant by its kindly light, all of us touch glory under its shade.

Any victory or fame is due to its grace. Any win is its will. All powerhouses are powered by it,

Man becomes a king or saint due to its kindness.

ब्रह्मैवेदममृतं पुरस्तादु ब्रह्म पश्चादु ब्रह्म दक्षिणतश्चोत्तरेण ।
अधश्चोर्ध्वं च प्रसृतं ब्रह्मैवेदं विश्वमिदं वरिष्ठम् ॥ २.२.११

brahmaivedamamṛtaṃ purastād brahma paścād brahma
dakṣiṇataścottareṇa | adhaścordhvaṃ ca prasṛtaṃ
brahmaivedaṃ viśvamidaṃ variṣṭham ॥ 2.2.11

ब्रह्म एव इदम् अमृतं पुरस्तात् ब्रह्म पश्चात् ब्रह्म दक्षिणतः च उत्तरेण ।
अधः च ऊर्ध्वं च प्रसृतं ब्रह्म एव इदं विश्वम् इदं वरिष्ठम् ॥

ब्रह्म $^{n1/1}$ Brahman एव ^{0} alone इदम् $^{n1/1}$ this अमृतं $^{n1/1}$ bliss,
पुरस्तात् ^{0} in front in space and time ब्रह्म $^{n1/1}$ Infinity
पश्चात् ^{0} behind in space and time ब्रह्म $^{n1/1}$ Infinity
दक्षिणतः ^{0} to the right च ^{0} and उत्तरेण ^{0} to left ।

अधः ^{0} below च ^{0} and ऊर्ध्वं ^{0} above च ^{0} and प्रसृतं $^{PPP\,n1/1}$
extended everywhere,
ब्रह्म $^{n1/1}$ Brahman एव ^{0} alone इदं $^{n1/1}$ this विश्वम् $^{n1/1}$ world,
इदं $^{n1/1}$ this वरिष्ठम् $^{n1/1}$ ultimate ॥

2.2.11 Mate - all of this, that, it, you and me are the
living examples of that immortal Brahman.

Brahman is in Front, it is behind, to the left and to the
right, my dear in the center of everything too. Up
above in the heavens is Brahman, down below in hell
as well.

The past was Divine, the future shall be Divine,
Wake up and see, the present too is perfect!

Whether you do right or you sense wrong, whether it
is the past history or the future in the making, it is all
willed, supervised, ordered and witnessed by
Brahman.

Let go of your obsession, loosen your scruffiness, and
wipe out your ill-will, Love alone rules, nay Light
alone is this magnificent universe.

Here ends the second year, filling the mind with awe,
clearing all the doubts, and establishing firm faith in the
good.

3rd Year 1st Semester

Life's last term doesn't ever end! It spills into the daily grind, it fashions the future.

Story Time

Now comes the story time. The best orator, the acclaimed speaker, the famous school; all give due attention to anecdote, entertainment, live examples, practical wisdom.

Story time. Lighten up fellas. Relax. Just sit back and enjoy the ride.

द्वा सुपर्णा सयुजा सखाया समानं वृक्षं परिषस्वजाते ।
तयोरन्यः पिप्पलं स्वाद्वत्त्यनश्नन्नन्यो अभिचाकशीति ॥ ३.१.१

tṛtīyaṃ muṇḍakam prathamaḥ khaṇḍaḥ
dvā suparṇā sayujā sakhāyā samānam vṛkṣam pariṣasvajāte
I tayoranyaḥ pippalam svādvattyanaśnannanyo

abhicākaśīti II 3.1.1

द्वा सुपर्णा सयुजा सखाया समानं वृक्षं परिषस्वजाते ।
तयोः अन्यः पिप्पलं स्वादु अत्ति अनश्नन् अन्यः अभिचाकशीति ॥

3.1.1 Nara and Narayana

Have you seen a tree teeming with birds and bees?
Have you spent any time tiptoeing in the woods?
Have you seen the stunning sunset? Or had pets and
fishes and friends?

What do you notice? What does the intellect see?

It is the same tree or school or workplace or village.
The sounds and delights and ambience is the same
for all.

Yet is each animal the same? Is each sibling satisfied
with the same toy?

One is quiet, reserved, content and shy. The other is
gregarious, outgoing, social and ambitious.

One sits calm, amused and nondescript, the other
aggressively pursues attention, cash backs and
rewards.

समाने वृक्षे पुरुषो निमग्नोऽनीशाया शोचति मुह्यमानः ।
जुष्टं यदा पश्यत्यन्यमीशमस्य महिमानमिति वीतशोकः ॥ ३.१.२
samāne vṛkṣe puruṣo nimagno'nīśayā śocati muhyamānaḥ I juṣṭaṃ yadā paśyatyanyamīśamasya mahimānamiti vītaśokaḥ ॥ 3.1.2

समाने वृक्षे पुरुषः निमग्नः अनीशाया शोचति मुह्यमानः ।
जुष्टं यदा पश्यति अन्यम् ईशाम् अस्य महिमानम् इति वीतशोकः ॥

3.1.2 And what happens after a while my friend?

After a life of toils and travails, having spent all energy running hither tither, having attained great rewards yet not the one that satiated the soul,

perchance one spots the wise in the vicinity.

One's inward eye is opened and one sees the calm co-traveller. The saint so near and accessible, a sight for sore eyes, and soothing like some heavenly balm.

One begins to experience Grace, one opens up to the ultimate embrace.

यदा पश्यः पश्यते रुक्मवर्णं कर्तारमीशं पुरुषं ब्रह्मयोनिम् ।
तदा विद्वान् पुण्यपापे विधूय निरञ्जनः परमं साम्यमुपैति ॥ ३.१.३
yadā paśyaḥ paśyate rukmavarṇam kartāramīśaṃ puruṣam brahmayonim | tadā vidvān puṇyapāpe vidhūya nirañjanaḥ paramaṃ sāmyamupaiti ‖ 3.1.3

यदा पश्यः पश्यते रुक्मवर्णं कर्तारम् ईशं पुरुषं ब्रह्मयोनिम् ।
तदा विद्वान् पुण्यपापे विधूय निरञ्जनः परमं साम्यम् उपैति ॥

यदा पश्यः पश्यते रुक्मवर्णं कर्तारमीशं पुरुषं ब्रह्मयोनिम् ।
तदा विद्वान् पुण्यपापे विधूय निरञ्जनः परमं साम्यमुपैति ॥ ३.१.३
yadā paśyaḥ paśyate rukmavarṇam kartāramīśaṃ puruṣam brahmayonim | tadā vidvān puṇyapāpe vidhūya nirañjanaḥ

3.1.3 We all seek inspiration. In the smallest trifling matter, we are looking for excitement, reward or appreciation.

Lo and behold, what then if Lord himself grants a vision. One look of his, one glimpse of Bliss, one experience of the highest, and then our life changes entirely.

No more then doth the mind crave after puny deprivations. No thought thence chases rotten pathways, nor does tongue get taste from druggy culture or kick from smoky sensations.

Lust gets erased from the heart, the knot of begging society for imagined or material gains loosens up.

Imperishable habits face instant closure, tendency to invite illness, destruction, shame loses steam.

Self-cheating and self-denial rupture apart; guilt, fear, blame and associated stains imposed on self and on society fade.

A human life is born.

प्राणो ह्येष यः सर्वभूतैर्विभाति विजानन् विद्वान् भवते नातिवादी ।
आत्मक्रीड आत्मरतिः क्रियावानेष ब्रह्मविदां वरिष्ठः ॥ ३.१.४

prāṇo hyeṣa yaḥ sarvabhūtairvibhāti vijānan vidvān
bhavate nātivādī | ātmakrīḍa ātmaratiḥ kriyāvāneṣa
brahmavidāṃ variṣṭhaḥ ॥ 3.1.4

प्राणः हि एषः यः सर्वभूतैः विभाति विजानन् विद्वान् भवते न अतिवादी
। आत्मक्रीडः आत्मरतिः क्रियावान् एष ब्रह्मविदां वरिष्ठः ॥
यः हि प्राणः एषः सर्वभूतैः विभाति इति विजानम् विद्वान् भवते
अतिवादी न भवते । एषः आत्मक्रीडः आत्मरतिः क्रियावान् ब्रह्मविदां
वरिष्ठः ॥

3.1.4 Human birth is indeed fragile, human birth is not of the body nor has anything to do with the physical.

In the famous American visa application they verify wealth - just how short-sighted can they get! And to verifying goodness they don't even try.

In some big muscular corporations they seek others extinction, sadly the plot has cast them using demonic neurons.

Well but what of the energy that courses through them, and what of the emotions that heave in my bosom? The wise declare it all is Brahman....

Soon you laugh, you split, you break up. Soon you embrace the Divine and acknowledge its dark shades. Soon it hits home that America and Afghanistan are both A grade and both are Brahman.

Sometimes you play the part of the hero, and sometimes of the heroine, both are one and the same Brahman. Only when the shaft hits bull's eye, only when the center is pierced, only when respect reverence and awe take charge of life Irrespective of news, views, analysis and observation, does enlightenment dawn. Such is the mysterious majestic life of the knowers of the Brahman.

सत्येन लभ्यस्तपसा ह्येष आत्मा सम्यग्ज्ञानेन ब्रह्मचर्येण नित्यम् ।
अन्तःशरीरे ज्योतिर्मयो हि शुभ्रो यं पश्यन्ति यतयः क्षीणदोषाः ॥
३.१.५

satyena labhyastapasā hyeṣa ātmā samyagjñānena
brahmacaryeṇa nityam | antaḥśarīre jyotirmayo hi śubhro
yaṃ paśyanti yatayaḥ kṣīṇadoṣāḥ ॥ 3.1.5

सत्येन लभ्यः तपसा हि एषः आत्मा सम्यग्ज्ञानेन ब्रह्मचर्येण नित्यम् ।
अन्तःशरीरे ज्योतिर्मयः हि शुभ्रः यं पश्यन्ति यतयः क्षीणदोषाः ॥
यं क्षीणदोषाः यतयः पश्यन्ति एषः ज्योतिर्मयः शुभ्रः आत्मा
अन्तःशरीरे हि सः नित्यम् सत्येन तपसा सम्यग्ज्ञानेन ब्रह्मचर्येण च
लभ्यः हि ॥

3.1.5 When both pain and pleasure are Brahman, when any trade practice, law or system has equal rating, what does one choose?

Up to you is easily said, but the brave wishes for courage, patience, kindness and discipline.

When white is pure and so is black and so also the whole gamut of intervening hues, can't one take any shade and go forward?

Trick question mate. Don't let it fool you.

When everyone is reveling in smoke and drink shouldn't you too take a bite? That is just sowing the seeds of a bitterly painful pitfall that will manifest after such a long time that you and your succeeding generation can never connect, and simply traverse the same destructive and unfulfilling trail again!

So much for theory, the story has become rather tacky.

Please clear this puzzling painting called Brahman.

The wise declare with all humility - yes all paths lead to Rome, any trick will get you there, eating sleeping entertaining and the short-lived thing called working are designed for each soul.

But if you are smart, if you are intelligent, if you are

seeking only the very best, then you shall with conscious effort embark on strengthening the core values common to all cultures and civilizations.

Friendliness, kindness, gentleness, caring, and sharing. You shall never then be tempted to fall prey to speaking ill. You shall be most careful to keep a strict watch on your tongue. You shall then never slander, abuse or spread gossip. You shall spend more and more time in a spiritual context,

That delights all, hurts few and radiates a deep sense of love, peace, and good-will.

This they declare as the sweetest path, filled with purifying grace.

सत्यमेव जयति नानृतं सत्येन पन्था विततो देवयानः ।
येनाक्रमन्त्यृषयो ह्याप्तकामा यत्र तत् सत्यस्य परमं निधानम् ॥ ३.१.६
satyameva jayati nānṛtaṃ satyena panthā vitato
devayānaḥ | yenākramanty ṛṣayo hyāptakāmā yatra tat
satyasya paramaṃ nidhānam || 3.1.6

सत्यम् एव जयति न अनृतं सत्येन पन्थाः विततः देवयानः । येन
आक्रमन्ति ऋषयः हि आप्तकामाः यत्र तत् सत्यस्य परमं निधानम् ॥

3.1.6 Truth Triumphs.

What of falsehood? Falsehood appears to win initially. Since both are inherent in Brahman, both seem to be victorious, albeit in different situations, at different times, or for different people.

Yet when wisdom dawns in life, one always takes the path of truth, one is not tempted by untruth.

Isn't this a bit muddy or tangential? Not at all, once you start tasting the rewards of truthfulness, the brave declare, you shall never ever be foiled by untruth. The path of truth takes a while to come into focus and it is the direct path to Brahman.

Untruth seems easy, attractive, and tempting, but after a long long time, it gets you thoroughly imprisoned, you fall terribly ill, and eke out a miserable existence. No doubt you reach Brahman, but such a path is not recommended.

In the end only the Truth wins. There is no contest, the honest win hands down.

बृहच्च तद् दिव्यमचिन्त्यरूपं सूक्ष्माच्च तत् सूक्ष्मतरं विभाति ।
दूरात् सुदूरे तदिहान्तिके च पश्यत्स्विहैव निहितं गुहायाम् ॥ ३.१.७
bṛhacca tad divyamacintyarūpaṃ sūkṣmācca tat
sūkṣmataraṃ vibhāti | dūrāt sudūre tadihāntike ca
paśyatsvihaiva nihitaṃ guhāyām ‖ 3.1.7

बृहत् च तत् दिव्यम् अचिन्त्यरूपं सूक्ष्मात् च तत् सूक्ष्मतरं विभाति ।
दूरात् सुदूरे तत् इह अन्तिके च पश्यत्सु इह एव निहितं गुहायाम् ॥

तत् बृहत् दिव्यम् अचिन्त्यरूपं च बिभाति। तत् सूक्ष्मात् सूक्ष्मतरं च
तत् दूरात् सुदूरे इह अन्तिके इह एव पश्यत्सु गुहायां निहितं च ॥

3.1.7 Since the path of righteousness is fraught with grave danger initially, no one understands or seeks it.

Since possibilities are immense, since opinions vary, since diverse schools propound contradictory tenets, it cannot be grasped by the faint- hearted.

The one without intense determination cannot unravel the complex equations leading to Brahman.

The lazy lethargic dull-headed is soon lost and mired in the maze of Brahman's staggering tempestuous networks, the weaklings get lured by its myriad dazzling lights and end up in a heap by the wayside.

For the one who never chooses to practice purity, the nondescript Brahman remains elusive till the very end.

He keeps searching for that one drop of nectar, he keeps begging to get his illness cured, but Brahman remains hidden. For he has never sought to open his own heart. He has never allowed grace to enter his dense brain.

न चक्षुषा गृह्यते नापि वाचा नान्यैर्देवैस्तपसा कर्मणा वा ।
ज्ञानप्रसादेन विशुद्धसत्त्वस्ततस्तु तं पश्यते निष्कलं ध्यायमानः ॥ ८

na cakṣuṣā gṛhyate nāpi vācā nānyairdevaistapasā karmaṇā
vā | jñānaprasādena viśuddhasattvastatastu taṃ paśyate
niṣkalaṃ dhyāyamānaḥ ॥ 3.1.8

न चक्षुषा गृह्यते न अपि वाचा न अन्यैः देवैः तपसा कर्मणाः वा ।
ज्ञानप्रसादेन विशुद्धसत्त्वः ततः तु तं पश्यते निष्कलं ध्यायमानः ॥
तत् आत्मतत्त्वं चक्षुषा न गृह्यते । वाचा अपि न । अनैः देवैः न । तपसा
कर्मणा वा न ज्ञानप्रसादेन विशुद्धसत्वः भवति ततः तु ध्यायमानः
निष्कलं तं पश्यते ॥

3.1.8 Why is it that it is forsaken by some stupid yet wealthy? Why is it that those whom the media chooses to highlight regularly get caught in material density?

Friend - our senses are not equipped to acknowledge it. Logic and reason fall flat trying to grapple with it. The fourth estate invests a lot on stories based on deception, greed, aggression or fanaticism, and the social media goes viral only when they spot someone's lame mistake. Remember all of this is few and far between, these are worst case examples that just happen. The majority is far unconnected, a wonder it pays willingly to read the stories!

How can those who hunger for outside news ever realize what's cooking within? When all the antennae are pointed outwards to snoop on unlucky neighbors, the space inside remains void and null. It cannot attain, nor can it welcome.

So friend only when you focus earnestly on Brahman, only when you reach out to Him, only when you Meditate and step within, can you glimpse love, can you taste Bliss, can you get established in secure wisdom.

एषोऽणुरात्मा चेतसा वेदितव्यो यस्मिन् प्राणः पञ्चधा संविवेश ।
प्राणैश्चित्तं सर्वमोतं प्रजानां यस्मिन् विशुद्धे विभवत्येष आत्मा ॥ ३.१.९

eṣo'ṇurātmā cetasā veditavyo yasmin prāṇaḥ pañcadhā saṃviveśa | prāṇaiścittaṃ sarvamotaṃ prajānāṃ yasmin viśuddhe vibhavatyeṣa ātmā ‖ 3.1.9

एषः अणुः आत्मा चेतसा वेदितव्यः यस्मिन् प्राणः पञ्चधा संविवेश ।
प्राणैः चित्तं सर्वम् ओतं प्रजानां यस्मिन् विशुद्धे विभवति एषः आत्मा ॥
एषः अणुः आत्मा चेतसा तस्मिन् शरीरे वेदितव्यः यस्मिन् प्राणः
पञ्चधा संविवेश । प्राणैः प्रजानाम् सर्वं चित्तम् ओतं यस्मिन् विशुद्धे एषः
आत्मा विभवति ॥

3.1.9 With regular sadhana, and Guruji's hollow and empty advance meditation courses, the workings of the vital life-force and its constituents - the 5 airs, viz. prana, apana, vyana, udana and samana get slowly revealed.

The para-sympathetic yogic practices that cause stress to be balanced in contrast with the sympathetic stress elevating systems of gymming and aerobics, also reveal the brain wave frequency spectrum to be composed of alpha, beta, gamma, Delta and Theta.

As this knowledge filters in, the 5 components of consciousness also become distinctly clear - sensuous mind, intellect, memory, ego and soul.

Then one's practices take a new turn of sincerity, regularity and priority. Thereby the heavy veil of ignorance gets worn and translucent, and the self-shines forth brightly.

This is known as direct experience of the pure soul.

यं यं लोकं मनसा संविभाति विशुद्धसत्त्वः कामयते यांश्च कामान् ।
तं तं लोकं जयते तांश्च कामांस्तस्मादात्मज्ञं ह्यर्चयेद् भूतिकामः ॥ १०

yaṃ yaṃ lokaṃ manasā saṃvibhāti viśuddhasattvaḥ kāmayate yāṃśca kāmān | taṃ taṃ lokaṃ jayate tāṃśca kāmāṃstasmādātmajñaṃ hyarcayed bhūtikāmaḥ || 3.1.10

यं यं लोकं मनसा संविभाति विशुद्धसत्त्वः कामयते यान् च कामान् ।
तं तं लोकं जयते तान् च कामान् तस्मात् आत्मज्ञं हि अर्चयेत्
भूतिकामः ॥

3.1.10 The saint endowed with such discrimination and soaked in the purity of dispassion, gets the upper hand on nature's energies. Its forces are then ever at his beck and call.

The physical laws bend to his wishes automatically, the primordial energies succumb to his laser-like mind that is free of conflict.

Hence anyone desirous of success must approach a Master with all humility and serve him, thereby ensuring self-growth, evolution and freedom.

Thus ends the 5th semester or the 1st part of the 3rd year, where the disciple learns the tools of the trade and gets to practice dispassion and meditation, and his faith is strengthened.

The Final Term

The living plane is sinusoidal in design. Also known as the karmic roller coaster. It is all relative or tangential here. Actually none is good, nothing and no one is bad. It is just a play of Divine and demonic energies, as we experience in the Hari Om Meditation. The Sanskrit word captures the essence far better, sur/asur without causing fear, turmoil, aggression. English being in its infancy, is still struggling to say things as they are, without adding the polarity, shade or spice of the reporter.

Some thrive on the crest, others like the trough, few balance in the middle.

After a while of resting and replenishing the thrill of excitement grips Brahman, some Sparks burst forth and escaping from its gravity, take birth in the sinusoidal plane - known by many names, the Relative, the Dvaita, the Leela, the Karmic.

It is rather a new beginning for all who land up here in the karmic. At the start of the 400 years lifespan, as children we are all the same, only the surrounding culture and societal fabric vary.

Freedom

The Guru has implicit faith in Brahman. He knows this is Brahman's play, direction, law and governance.

The realized soul lives in total acceptance. It is an acceptance that is un-tamperable. When the intellect has become soft like butter, and regular Sadhana keeps the citta free of troublesome memories, then a moment dawns when nature's energies, physical laws, and man-made events lose all potential in his presence. In other words the forces become calm, placid, and undisturbing for him.

That is the reason the Guru moves free. He does not despise anyone. He has no fear of natural calamity. He has not an iota of doubt.

The Guru's focus and determination are so strong and his identification with Brahman so total that he begins to consider all as holy and sacred. He reveres all, denies none.

This makes his aura luminous and it resonates far and wide. Humans, animals, trees, and rivers become his friends. Seasons are easy on him, illness too doesn't bother much.

This is the story of Nirvana, freedom.

स वेदैतत् परमं ब्रह्म धाम यत्र विश्वं निहितं भाति शुभ्रम् ।
उपासते पुरुषं ये ह्यकामास्ते शुक्रमेतदतिवर्तन्ति धीराः ॥ ३.२.१

sa vedaitat paramaṃ brahma dhāma yatra viśvaṃ nihitaṃ bhāti śubhram | upāsate puruṣaṃ ye hyakāmāste śukrametadativartanti dhīrāḥ ॥ 3.2.1

सः वेद एतत् परमं ब्रह्म धाम यत्र विश्वं निहितं भाति शुभ्रम् ।
उपासते पुरुषं ये हि अकामाः ते शुक्रम् एतत् अतिवर्तन्ति धीराः ॥
सः एतत् परमं ब्रह्म धाम वेद यत्र विश्वं निहितं यं च शुभ्रं भाति। ये अकामाः पुरुषम् उपासते ते धीराः एतत् शुक्रं अतिवर्तन्ति हि ॥

3.2.1 This is the means to attain enlightenment.

Those brave souls who take the path of regularity in Sadhana, Satsang, Silence and proper diet, become bereft of superfluous needs and wants.

Moods and emotions become benevolent, desires become trifles.

In time their steadfastness attains the point of total power matching. After they have made their mark in the world, after they have balanced the forces of good and evil, they journey forth to the plane free of old age, sickness, lack.

They simply ascend the ramp since their aura matches its potential. That plane is also called the plane of absolute Brahman.

कामान् यः कामयते मन्यमानः स कामभिर्जायते तत्र तत्र ।
पर्याप्तकामस्य कृतात्मनस्तु इहैव सर्वे प्रविलीयन्ति कामाः ॥ ३.२.२
kāmān yaḥ kāmayate manyamānaḥ sa kāmabhirjāyate
tatra tatra | paryāptakāmasya kṛtātmanastu ihaiva sarve
pravilīyanti kāmāḥ ॥ 3.2.2

कामान् यः कामयते मन्यमानः सः कामभिः जायते तत्र तत्र ।
पर्याप्तकामस्य कृतात्मनः तु इह एव सर्वे प्रविलीयन्ति कामाः ॥

3.2.2 In case we have changed the body within the 400 year span, then as children we shall be born with some genetic traits from the previous lifetimes. These so called karmic impressions will make us susceptible to behave and speak and act in a specific manner when faced with a person or situation.

However this is only a probability, determined by how strong the impressions are and how big a challenge the current moment poses. In case we get lucky to come to Guruji with an open mind, then his teachings, especially the Sudarshan Kriya, will just erase those impressions, or make them quite faint in the very least. Then the journey of the remaining 400 years will not only become delightful, productive, and graceful, it shall also rub off on those we interact with and make their flight smooth.

Such souls then may go back to the source or plane of Bliss sooner than 400 years, or wish to play longer and retire only at the end of 400 years.

In any case, even those who fail to adopt a value system or ingrain some healthy discipline, attain Brahman at the end of 400 years. Only their total lifespan shall have a lot of grief and suffering, too much turmoil, blemish or shame. Not to worry, since some souls have been seen to have such proclivity, As you sow so shall you reap.

नायमात्मा प्रवचनेन लभ्यो न मेधया न बहुना श्रुतेन ।
यमेवैष वृणुते तेन लभ्यस्तस्यैष आत्मा विवृणुते तनुं स्वाम् ॥ ३.२.३
nāyamātmā pravacanena labhyo na medhayā na bahunā śrutena | yamevaiṣa vṛṇute tena labhyastasyaiṣa ātmā vivṛṇute tanuṃ svām ॥ 3.2.3

न अयम् आत्मा प्रवचनेन लभ्यः न मेधया न बहुना श्रुतेन ।
यम् एव एष वृणुते तेन लभ्यः तस्य एषः आत्मा विवृणुते तनुं स्वाम् ॥

अयम् आत्मा प्रवचनेन न लभ्यः न मेधया न बहुना श्रुतेन यम् एव एषः वृणुते। तेन लभ्यः तस्य एषः आत्मा स्वां तनुं विवृणुते ॥

3.2.3 A big bouncer is hurled at so called fanatics who lean to extreme righteousness or strict religiousness or other harsh Puritan measures.

This Brahman does not favor lengthy discourses, it does not filter into cutting edge intellect, crazy genius, or prodigal sons. It is not revealed by rote learning of any text, philosophy, or methodology.

Only the brave soul willing to take responsibility with a cheerful heart and Open mind is whom Brahman favors.

The key is discipline with a joyful acceptance of every experience and an openness that keeps the mind flexible for Brahman's entry.

Evenness of temper, tranquility of emotion, a heart free of rigid obsessiveness, these are the qualities Brahman manifests in.

Fitness of both mind and body, pleasant countenance, balance in diet and exercise, refraining from harsh, bitter, or mocking speech, such aspects are most conducive for Brahman's welcome.

नायमात्मा बलहीनेन लभ्यो न च प्रमादात् तपसो वाप्यलिङ्गात् ।
एतैरुपायैर्यतते यस्तु विद्वांस्तस्यैष आत्मा विशते ब्रह्मधाम ॥ ३.२.४
nāyamātmā balahīnena labhyo na ca pramādāt tapaso
vāpyaliṅgāt | etairupāyairyatate yastu vidvāṃstasyaiṣa
ātmā viśate brahmadhāma ॥ 3.2.4

न अयम् आत्मा बलहीनेन लभ्यः न च प्रमादात् तपसः वा अपि
अलिङ्गात् । एतैः उपायैः यतते यः तु विद्वान् तस्य एषः आत्मा विशते
ब्रह्मधाम ॥

अयम् आत्मा बलहीनेन न लभ्यः प्रमादात् च न वा अलिङ्गात् तपसः
अपि न लभ्यः यः विद्वान् एतैः उपायैः यतते तस्य एषः आत्मा
ब्रह्मधाम विशते ॥

3.2.4 Most theories emphasize mental clarity and skillset, however that additionally needs a supple mind, a strong frame, and a loving heart, to qualify for Brahman.

When we see a healthy baby, we feel overjoyed. When we see a robust personality, it evokes confidence. A fit body has perhaps been overlooked by some theoretical physicists and armchair orators, so the Master quells it.

Another point to beware of is logic in excess or profane logic or illogical reasoning. Such a mindset has firmly shut the doors to Brahman.

Also body torture, unpleasant antics, destructive rituals lead one nowhere. Any practice that is only slanted to draw attention or create commotion is far removed from Brahman.

At the same time the ordinary man who does not gossip, refrains from rumor mongering, pursues his own honest duty, and maintains his civility and gentleness, gets easy access to Brahman.

सम्प्राप्यैनम् ऋषयो ज्ञानतृप्ताः कृतात्मानो वीतरागाः प्रशान्ताः
ते सर्वगं सर्वतः प्राप्य धीरा युक्तात्मानः सर्वमेवाविशन्ति ॥ ३.२.५

samprāpyainam ṛṣayo jñānatṛptāḥ kṛtātmāno vītarāgāḥ
praśāntāḥ te sarvagaṃ sarvataḥ prāpya dhīrā yuktātmānaḥ
sarvamevāviśanti ॥ 3.2.5

सम्प्राप्य एनम् ऋषयः ज्ञानतृप्ताः कृतात्मानः वीतरागाः प्रशान्ताः
ते सर्वगं सर्वतः प्राप्य धीराः युक्तात्मानः सर्वम् एव आविशन्ति ॥
एनम् सम्प्राप्य ऋषयः ज्ञानतृप्ताः कृतात्मानः वीतरागाः प्रशान्ताः
भवन्ति ते युक्तात्मानः धीराः सर्वगं सर्वतः प्राप्य सर्वम् एव आविशन्ति
॥

3.2.5 Sages who find resonance with Brahman attain samadhana, a deep contentment. Gratefulness becomes evident in their behavior, and serenity reflects on their face.

Likes and dislikes no longer categorize them, affability and grace exude from them.

These Yogis, brave adventurers committed to the truth, their every cell infused with strong faith, their entire being brimming with Divine embrace, Own the great Brahman with open arms, and immerse themselves fully in the Oneness.

This is an experience par excellence, this is a journey beyond rewards, this is what the pure heart longs for, this is the fondest dream.

वेदान्तविज्ञानसुनिश्चितार्थाः संन्यासयोगाद् यतयः शुद्धसत्त्वाः ।
ते ब्रह्मलोकेषु परान्तकाले परामृताः परिमुच्यन्ति सर्वे ॥ ३.२.६
This verse is frequently chanted to welcome a saint.

vedāntavijñānasuniścitārthāḥ saṃnyāsayogād yatayaḥ
śuddhasattvāḥ | te brahmalokeṣu parāntakāle parāmṛtāḥ
parimucyanti sarve || 3.2.6

वेदान्त–विज्ञान–सुनिश्चितार्थाः संन्यास–योगात् यतयः शुद्ध–सत्त्वाः ।
ते ब्रह्म–लोकेषु परान्तकाले परामृताः परिमुच्यन्ति सर्वे ॥

3.2.6 The greatest adventurers, the brilliant entrepreneurs, the artists deeply connected to their art, the cheerful sportsmen, happy-go-lucky school children, doting mothers and the perfect yogis, they all have the stamp of Brahman.

They all thrive in Brahman, and with joyful harmony live their lives.

Folk around them sense the soothing aura they radiate, all feel blessed in their presence. Many claim they help fulfill aspirations, wishes, dreams! Why not, when you feel good, certainly your performance raises and your efforts fructify.

Their dropping of the body is so calm and peaceful, their onwards journey is marked with happy composure, the whole world celebrates their liberation.

गताः कलाः पञ्चदश प्रतिष्ठा देवाश्च सर्वे प्रतिदेवतासु ।
कर्माणि विज्ञानमयश्च आत्मा परेऽव्यये सर्व एकीभवन्ति ॥ ३.२.७

gatāḥ kalāḥ pañcadaśa pratiṣṭhā devāśca sarve pratidevatāsu | karmāṇi vijñānamayaśca ātmā pare'vyaye sarva ekībhavanti ॥ 3.2.7

गताः कलाः पञ्चदश प्रतिष्ठा देवाः च सर्वे प्रतिदेवतासु ।
कर्माणि विज्ञानमयः च आत्मा परे अव्यये सर्वे एकी–भवन्ति ॥

पञ्चदश = fifteenth, पञ्चदशः = fifteen

3.2.7 The 5 senses, 5 organs of action, and the 5 objects to which the senses get drawn, i.e. the 5 elements - Earth, water, air, light and space, these 15 gross constituents of the body-mind complex get freed from their moorings at the time of passing of the soul from the karmic plane to the blissful plane.

Before the end of the 400 year average timespan, they dissolve in Brahman since no impressions remain for a new body to clothe the soul. (Of course their will to play further and be reborn is always granted if that be the case).

The subtle body responsible for the functions
- of the central nervous system,
- the autonomous respiration, etc.,
- the luminous thought and emotion generating mechanisms,
- citta and ego sacs,

all of these subtle energies also bid adieu from the brave soul.

That soul is then ideally pure and without any cover or color, so its merger with Brahman is total and indistinguishable.

यथा नद्यः स्यन्दमानाः समुद्रेऽस्तं गच्छन्ति नामरूपे विहाय ।
तथा विद्वान् नामरूपाद् विमुक्तः परात्परं पुरुषमुपैति दिव्यम् ॥ ३.२.८
yathā nadyaḥ syandamānāḥ samudre'staṃ gacchanti
nāmarūpe vihāya | tathā vidvān nāmarūpād vimuktaḥ
parātparaṃ puruṣamupaiti divyam || 3.2.8

यथा नद्यः स्यन्दमानाः समुद्रे अस्तं गच्छन्ति नामरूपे विहाय ।
तथा विद्वान् नामरूपात् विमुक्तः परात् परं पुरुषम् उपैति दिव्यम् ॥

3.2.8 Even as springs and tributaries and rivers race gleefully to unite with the ocean where their limited identifications are all erased and the union is total,

And no more inside the ocean can anyone then name the original streams, nor sense the original color, flavor, or taste,

So also do the liberated souls get united with Brahman. **(Please do not forget that all of us too eventually do the same)**. The words - liberated, brave, saintly etc., simply refer to their existence when alive in body as joyous, free, pure. Compared to that the existence of the common populace has a two-fold difference.

1. The highs and lows are intense and create much heat, friction, and strong impression. The overall quality of life is poor, shoddy, unenviable.
2. For sure the ride shall span 400 years, in extreme cases 800. And that too just imagine - filled with pain, misery, illness, crashed relationships, a fearful horror show.

A question may be asked - if the soul remains impure at the end of 400 years how can it merge with Brahman? Mate - it is due to the time principle.

All of us who do Nadi Shodana Pranayama, have heard the instruction - 9 rounds or 5 minutes at least.

In plain words the Pranayama ends in 5 minutes, whether you do it correctly or incorrectly.

That is Brahman's working, after a certain time everything dissolves, the movie ends, all actors retire backstage.

A new script is then enacted from scratch. In it the previous villain might play the hero, the earlier heroine might be some hapless maid.

The river example includes pure waters, sullen tributaries, muddy streams, dangerous gorges, foul drains, placid seas.

स यो ह वै तत् परमं ब्रह्म वेद ब्रह्मैव भवति नास्याब्रह्मवित् कुले भवति । तरति शोकं तरति पाप्मानं गुहाग्रन्थिभ्यो विमुक्तोऽमृतो भवति ॥ ३.२.९

sa yo ha vai tat paramaṃ brahma veda brahmaiva bhavati nāsyābrahmavit kule bhavati | tarati śokaṃ tarati pāpmānaṃ guhāgranthibhyo vimukto'mṛto bhavati || 3.2.9

सः यः ह वै तत् परमं ब्रह्म वेद ब्रह्म एव भवति न अस्य अब्रह्मवित् कुले भवति । तरति शोकं तरति पाप्मानं गुहा–ग्रन्थिभ्यः विमुक्तः अमृतः भवति ॥

3.2.9 A soul that attains Brahman well in time is highly regarded. His stories are sung, his exploits become legendary, books are filled with his glory.

Many philosophies are propounded concerning him, many people seek to emulate him. Many assume his ownership, many claim him ancestor.

The one amongst us who reaches Brahman first is treated as God. That is why God is worshipped in so many names and forms all over the world. That one Brahman is mistaken to have a particular body, race, religion or set of attributes.

A hero is honored by some, others laud someone else, possibly many are unaware of the two!

Brahman is difficult to typify, it doesn't fully fit any known person, entity or idol, yet it is definitely all. All are his subsets, all attributes are his.

Many unknown unsung heroes, saints, divine souls roam the planet. Their chief quality is a loving, accepting, large heart.

One may become quite balanced and pragmatic in day to day living, but one is really tested in the extreme circumstances.

The one who allows the wickedest event to pass without causing bitter impression, nay who offers his profuse thanks to the almighty that he was chosen for the cruel storm, he alone is said to have untied all the knots in the heart. He alone has become soft as Brahman while still in body.

This stage is referred to as the immortal existence.

Immortality refers to the fact you are no longer trying to duck, prevent, escape or be in any sort of blockage or denial.

तदेतद् ऋचाऽभ्युक्तम् । क्रियावन्तः श्रोत्रिया ब्रह्मनिष्ठाः स्वयं जुह्वत एकर्षिं श्रद्दयन्तः । तेषामेवैतां ब्रह्मविद्यां वदेत शिरोव्रतं विधिवद् यैस्तु चीर्णम् ॥ ३.२.१०

tadetad ṛcā'bhyuktam | kriyāvantaḥ śrotriyā brahmaniṣṭhāḥ svayaṃ juhvata ekarṣiṃ śraddhayantaḥ | teṣāmevaitāṃ brahmavidyāṃ vadeta śirovrataṃ vidhivad yaistu cīrṇam ॥ 3.2.10

तत् एतत् ऋचा अभ्युक्तम् । क्रियावन्तः श्रोत्रियाः ब्रह्मनिष्ठाः स्वयं जुह्वते एकर्षिं श्रद्दयन्तः । तेषाम् एव एतान् ब्रह्मविद्यां वदेत शिरोव्रतं विधिवत् यैः तु चीर्णम् ॥

3.2.10 Clean Shaven, head Shaven too. Mundaka. The monk with clarity of vision, no cloudiness. The man with nothing to hide in his beard. The soul with an ego that is light, a memory that is untainted. A Shave, as in handsome, shining, clean, pure. Innocent as a New born.

That is why our Advance Meditation Course AMC is called a journey - From the Head to the Heart.

A soul who is committed to AMC with a yogic attitude, with fairness and non-prejudice, easily shakes off all burdens of the head, becomes a Mundaka.

This Upanishad makes sense to such a soul. This teaching finds favor in his heart. He benefits the maximum. So says a verse in the Rigveda. It qualifies the aspirant. That is the minimum requirement.

Sitting at the Master's feet, attending his satsang regularly, listening to his discourse again and again, and keeping the mind open, the heart loving, all of this shall get you there. One-pointed commitment, the fire of passionate devotion, is the key.

Arise, Awake and Joyfully imbibe this ultimate wisdom. Prioritize to Purify thyself. The Divine is yours, Brahman is yours, Nature's forces are here to serve you.

तदेतत् सत्यम् ऋषिरङ्गिराः पुरोवाच नैतदचीर्णव्रतोऽधीते ।
नमः परमऋषिभ्यो नमः परमऋषिभ्यः ॥ ३.२.११

tadetat satyam ṛṣiraṅgirāḥ purovāca
naitadacīrṇavrato'dhīte | namaḥ paramarṣibhyo namaḥ
paramarṣibhyaḥ ॥ 3.2.11

तत् एतत् सत्यम् ऋषिः अङ्गिराः पुरा उवाच न एतत् अचीर्णव्रतः
अधीते । नमः परम–ऋषिभ्यः नमः परम–ऋषिभ्यः ॥

3.2.11 Thus is recorded the Upanishad that was revealed by the great sage Angiras in the olden days.

Such is the wisdom that emanated from the one whose body was filled with nectar. Whose heart was the cradle of God. Whose limbs were fit to hold the fiery Kundalini. Whose speech was concise, convincing, and respectful.

It is pointless to discuss it without reference or proper guidance. It becomes irrelevant for the naive, for one lacking time or focus it carries no appeal. It is so fine and soft that it causes no ripple in a stormy mind. A blocked heart lacking the will should first be prepared with a routine of proper diet, exercise, and basic education.

Step by step must one be led. For the contented and sincere must it be shared with.

Salutations to the Great seers. Prostrations to the Divine sages.

Deepest appreciation and grateful acknowledgement to the indomitable Rishis.

Jai Gurudev. 1:31pm. Monday after Rudram chanting, a full belly, and a fantastic sunny January day. 1:33pm

Etymology of Upanishad

व्युत्पत्ति
Consider Adi Shankaracharya's derivation of the word 'Upanishad' as given in his bhashyam on the Katha Upanishad.

उप + नि + षद् + क्विप् –> उपनिषद्

The Sanskrit root from Dhatupatha 1c - 854, 6c - 1427 षद्ऌ विशरण–गति–अवसादनेषु has the three meanings, namely विशरण= wither, गति= attain, अवसादनं = sit.

In the context of wisdom, we can say
- wither away one's stupidity
- attain liberation
- sit with a conviction

The upasarga उप stands for nearness, closeness.
The upasarga नि stands for delving into, intense
The pratyaya क्विप् makes a noun, and while joining, it vanishes entirely.

Thus the word 'Upanishad' is formed, and it has the meaning of destroying one's ignorance and gaining freedom, when we sit devotedly at the feet of the Master.

Latin Transliteration Chart

International Alphabet of Sanskrit Transliteration (I.A.S.T.)

a	ā	i	ī	u	ū	ṛ	ṝ		ḷ	
अ	आ	इ	ई	उ	ऊ	ऋ	ॠ		ऌ	
						◌ृ	◌ॄ		◌ॢ	
e	ai	o	au	ṃ	m̐	ḥ	Ardha Visarga		oṃ	
ए	ऐ	ओ	औ	◌ं	◌ँ	◌ः	□		ॐ	

Consonants are shown with vowel 'a= अ' for uttering										
ka	क	ca	च	ṭa	ट	ta	त		pa	प
kha	ख	cha	छ	ṭha	ठ	tha	थ		pha	फ
ga	ग	ja	ज	ḍa	ड	da	द		ba	ब
gha	घ	jha	झ	ḍha	ढ	dha	ध		bha	भ
ṅa	ङ	ña	ञ	ṇa	ण	na	न		ma	म
ya	ra	la	va		ḷa	'				
य	र	ल	व		ळ	S				
			Consonant only							
śa	ṣa	sa	ha		ka	क्अ = क				
श	ष	स	ह		k	क्				

The symbol ꣳ is pronounced as गुं guṃ. It is an ayogavaha अयोगवाह sound seen in Vedic literature due to Sandhi.

Verses for Chanting with Svaras

Accents used in Sanskrit verses increase the power and flow of the mantras during chanting.

Anudatta ◌॒ = अनुदात्तः = signifies base pitch.

Udatta = उदात्तः = unmarked, standard pitch.

Svarita ॑ = स्वरितः = high pitch.

Dirgha Svarita ॒॑ = दीर्घः स्वरितः = high to low to standard pitch.

॥ अथ अथर्ववेदीय मुण्डकोपनिषद् ॥

शान्तिपाठः

ॐ भद्रं कर्णेभिः शृणुयाम देवाः । भद्रं पश्येम आक्षभिर्यजत्राः । स्थिरैरङ्गैस् तुष्टुवाꣳ सस्तनूभिः । व्यशेम देवहितं यदायुः । स्वस्ति न इन्द्रो वृद्धश्रवाः । स्वस्ति नः पूषा विश्ववेदाः । स्वस्ति नस्ताक्ष्र्यो अरिष्टनेमिः । स्वस्ति नो बृहस्पतिर्दधातु ॥ ॐ शान्तिः शान्तिः शान्तिः ॥

प्रथममुण्डकं प्रथमः खण्डः

ॐ ब्रह्मा देवानां प्रथमः सम्बभूव विश्वस्य कर्ता भुवनस्य गोप्ता ।
स ब्रह्मविद्यां सर्वविद्याप्रतिष्ठामथर्वाय ज्येष्ठपुत्राय प्राह ॥ १.१.१
अथर्वणे यां प्रवदेत ब्रह्माथर्वा तां पुरोवाचाङ्गिरे ब्रह्मविद्याम् ।
स भारद्वाजाय सत्यवहाय प्राह भारद्वाजोऽङ्गिरसे परावराम् ॥ १.१.२
शौनको ह वै महाशालोऽङ्गिरसं विधिवदुपसन्नः पप्रच्छ ।
कस्मिन् नु भगवो विज्ञाते सर्वमिदं विज्ञातं भवतीति ॥ १.१.३
तस्मै स होवाच । द्वे विद्ये वेदितव्ये इति ह स्म यद् ब्रह्मविदो वदन्ति परा चैवापरा च ॥ १.१.४

तत्रापरा ऋग्वेदो यजुर्वेदः सामवेदोऽथर्ववेदः शिक्षा कल्पो व्याकरणं निरुक्तं छन्दो ज्योतिषमिति । अथ परा यया तदक्षरमधिगम्यते ॥ १.१.५
यत् तदद्रेश्यमग्राह्यमगोत्रमवर्णमचक्षुःश्रोत्रं तदपाणिपादम् ।

नित्यं विभुं सर्वगतं सुसूक्ष्मं तदव्ययं यद् भूतयोनिं परिपश्यन्ति धीराः ॥ १.१.६

यथोर्णनाभिः सृजते गृह्णते च यथा पृथिव्यामोषधयः सम्भवन्ति ।

यथा सतः पुरुषात् केशलोमानि तथाक्षरात् सम्भवतीह विश्वम् ॥ १.१.७

तपसा चीयते ब्रह्म ततोऽन्नमभिजायते ।

अन्नात् प्राणो मनः सत्यं लोकाः कर्मसु चामृतम् ॥ १.१.८

यः सर्वज्ञः सर्वविद् यस्य ज्ञानमयं तपः ।

तस्मादेतद् ब्रह्म नाम रूपमन्नं च जायते ॥ १.१.९

प्रथममुण्डकं द्वितीयः खण्डः

तदेतत् सत्यं मन्त्रेषु कर्माणि कवयो यान्यपश्यंस्तानि त्रेतायां बहुधा सन्ततानि । तान्याचरथ नियतं सत्यकामा एष वः पन्थाः सुकृतस्य लोके॥१.२.१

यदा लेलायते ह्यर्चिः समिद्धे हव्यवाहने ।

तदाऽऽज्यभागावन्तरेणाऽऽहुतीः प्रतिपादयेत् ॥ १.२.२

यस्याग्निहोत्रमदर्शमपौर्णमासमचातुर्मास्यमनाग्रयणमतिथिवर्जितं च ।

अहुतमवैश्वदेवमविधिना हुतमासप्तमांस्तस्य लोकान् हिनस्ति ॥ १.२.३

काली कराली च मनोजवा च सुलोहिता या च सुधूम्रवर्णा ।

स्फुलिङ्गिनी विश्वरुची च देवी लेलायमाना इति सप्त जिह्वाः ॥ १.२.४

एतेषु यश्चरते भ्राजमानेषु यथाकालं चाऽऽहुतयो ह्याददायन् ।

तं नयन्त्येताः सूर्यस्य रश्मयो यत्र देवानां पतिरेकोऽधिवासः ॥ १.२.५

एह्येहीति तमाहुतयः सुवर्चसः सूर्यस्य रश्मिभिर्यजमानं वहन्ति ।

प्रियां वाचमभिवदन्त्योऽर्चयन्त्य एष वः पुण्यः सुकृतो ब्रह्मलोकः ॥ १.२.६

प्लवा ह्येते अदृढा यज्ञरूपा अष्टादशोक्तमवरं येषु कर्म ।

एतच्छ्रेयो येऽभिनन्दन्ति मूढा जरामृत्युं ते पुनरेवापि यन्ति ॥ १.२.७

अविद्यायामन्तरे वर्तमानाः स्वयं धीराः पण्डितं मन्यमानाः ।

जङ्घन्यमानाः परियन्ति मूढा अन्धेनैव नीयमाना यथान्धाः ॥ १.२.८

अविद्यायां बहुधा वर्तमाना वयं कृतार्था इत्यभिमन्यन्ति बालाः ।

यत् कर्मिणो न प्रवेदयन्ति रागात् तेनातुराः क्षीणलोकाश्च्यवन्ते ॥ १.२.९

इष्टापूर्तं मन्यमाना वरिष्ठं नान्यच्छ्रेयो वेदयन्ते प्रमूढाः ।

नाकस्य पृष्ठे ते सुकृतेऽनुभूत्वेमं लोकं हीनतरं वा विशन्ति ॥ १.२.१०

तपःश्रद्धे ये ह्युपवसन्त्यरण्ये शान्ता विद्वांसो भैक्ष्यचर्यां चरन्तः ।

सूर्यद्वारेण ते विरजाः प्रयान्ति यत्रामृतः स पुरुषो ह्यव्ययात्मा ॥ १.२.११

परीक्ष्य लोकान् कर्मचितान् ब्राह्मणो निर्वेदमायान्नास्त्यकृतः कृतेन ।

तद्विज्ञानार्थं स गुरुमेवाभिगच्छेत् समित्पाणिः श्रोत्रियं ब्रह्मनिष्ठम् ॥ १.२.१२

तस्मै स विद्वानुपसन्नाय सम्यक् प्रशान्तचित्ताय शमान्विताय ।

येनाक्षरं पुरुषं वेद सत्यं प्रोवाच तां तत्त्वतो ब्रह्मविद्याम् ॥ १.२.१३

द्वितीयमुण्डकं प्रथमः खण्डः

तदेतत् सत्यं यथा सुदीप्तात् पावकाद् विस्फुलिङ्गाः सहस्रशः प्रभवन्ते सरूपाः

। तथाऽक्षराद् विविधाः सौम्य भावाः प्रजायन्ते तत्र चैवापि यन्ति ॥ २.१.१

दिव्यो ह्यमूर्तः पुरुषः सबाह्याभ्यन्तरो ह्यजः ।

अप्राणो ह्यमनाः शुभ्रो ह्यक्षरात् परतः परः ॥ २.१.२

एतस्माज्जायते प्राणो मनः सर्वेन्द्रियाणि च ।

खं वायुज्र्योतिरापः पृथिवी विश्वस्य धारिणी ॥ २.१.३

अग्निर्मूर्धा चक्षुषी चन्द्रसूर्यौ दिशः श्रोत्रे वाग् विवृताश्च वेदाः ।

वायुः प्राणो हृदयं विश्वमस्य पद्भ्यां पृथिवी ह्येष सर्वभूतान्तरात्मा ॥ २.१.४

तस्मादग्निः समिधो यस्य सूर्यः सोमात् पर्जन्य ओषधयः पृथिव्याम् ।

पुमान् रेतः सिञ्चति योषितायां बह्वीः प्रजाः पुरुषात् सम्प्रसूताः ॥ २.१.५

तस्माद् ऋचः साम यजूंषि दीक्षा यज्ञाश्च सर्वे क्रतवो दक्षिणाश्च ।

संवत्सरश्च यजमानश्च लोकाः सोमो यत्र पवते यत्र सूर्यः ॥ २.१.६

तस्माच्च देवा बहुधा सम्प्रसूताः साध्या मनुष्याः पशवो वयांसि ।

प्राणापानौ व्रीहियवौ तपश्च श्रद्धा सत्यं ब्रह्मचर्यं विधिश्च ॥ २.१.७

सप्त प्राणाः प्रभवन्ति तस्मात् सप्तार्चिषः समिधः सप्त होमाः ।

सप्त इमे लोका येषु चरन्ति प्राणा गुहाशया निहिताः सप्त सप्त ॥ २.१.८

अतः समुद्रा गिरयश्च सर्वेऽस्मात् स्यन्दन्ते सिन्धवः सर्वरूपाः ।

अतश्च सर्वा ओषधयो रसश्च येनैष भूतैस्तिष्ठते ह्यन्तरात्मा ॥ २.१.९

पुरुष एवेदं विश्वं कर्म तपो ब्रह्म परामृतम् ।

एतद् यो वेद निहितं गुहायां सोऽविद्याग्रन्थिं विकिरतीह सोम्य ॥ २.१.१०

<u>द्वितीयमुण्डकं द्वितीयः खण्डः</u>

आविः सन्निहितं गुहाचरन्नाम महत् पदमत्रैतत् समर्पितम् । एजत्

प्राणन्निमिषच्च यदेतज्जानथ सदसद्वरेण्यं परं विज्ञानाद् यद् वरिष्ठं प्रजानाम् ॥

२.२.१

यदर्चिमद्यदणुभ्योऽणु च यस्मिँल्लोका निहिता लोकिनश्च । तदेतदक्षरं ब्रह्म स

प्राणस्तदु वाङ् मनः । तदेतत् सत्यं तदमृतं तद् वेद्धव्यं सोम्य विद्धि ॥ २.२.२

धनुर्गृहीत्वौपनिषदं महास्त्रं शरं ह्युपासानिशितं सन्धयीत ।

आयम्य तद् भावगतेन चेतसा लक्ष्यं तदेवाक्षरं सोम्य विद्धि ॥ २.२.३

प्रणवो धनुः शरो ह्यात्मा ब्रह्म तल्लक्ष्यमुच्यते ।

अप्रमत्तेन वेद्धव्यं शरवत् तन्मयो भवेत् ॥ २.२.४

यस्मिन् द्यौः पृथिवी चान्तरिक्षमोतं मनः सह प्राणैश्च सर्वैः ।

तमेवैकं जानथ आत्मानमन्या वाचो विमुञ्चथामृतस्यैष सेतुः ॥ २.२.५

अरा इव रथनाभौ संहता यत्र नाड्यः स एषोऽन्तश्चरते बहुधा जायमानः ।

ॐ इत्येवं ध्यायथ आत्मानं स्वस्ति वः पाराय तमसः परस्तात् ॥ २.२.६

यः सर्वज्ञः सर्वविद् यस्यैष महिमा भुवि । दिव्ये ब्रह्मपुरे ह्येष व्योम्न्यात्मा

प्रतिष्ठितः । मनोमयः प्राणशरीरनेता प्रतिष्ठितोऽन्ने हृदयं सन्निधाय ।

तद् विज्ञानेन परिपश्यन्ति धीरा आनन्दरूपममृतं यद् विभाति ॥ २.२.७

भिद्यते हृदयग्रन्थिश्छिद्यन्ते सर्वसंशयाः ।

क्षीयन्ते चास्य कर्माणि तस्मिन् दृष्टे परावरे ॥ २.२.८

हिरण्मये परे कोशे विरजं ब्रह्म निष्कलम् ।

तच्छुभ्रं ज्योतिषां ज्योतिस्तद् यदात्मविदो विदुः ॥ २.२.९

न तत्र सूर्यो भाति न चन्द्रतारकं नेमा विद्युतो भान्ति कुतोऽयमग्निः ।

तमेव भान्तमनुभाति सर्वं तस्य भासा सर्वमिदं विभाति ॥ २.२.१०

ब्रह्मैवेदममृतं पुरस्ताद् ब्रह्म पश्चाद् ब्रह्म दक्षिणतश्चोत्तरेण ।

अधश्चोर्ध्वं च प्रसृतं ब्रह्मैवेदं विश्वमिदं वरिष्ठम् ॥ २.२.११

तृतीयमुण्डकं प्रथमः खण्डः

द्वा सुपर्णा सयुजा सखाया समानं वृक्षं परिषस्वजाते ।

तयोरन्यः पिप्पलं स्वाद्वत्त्यनश्नन्नन्यो अभिचाकशीति ॥ ३.१.१

समाने वृक्षे पुरुषो निमग्नोऽनीशया शोचति मुह्यमानः ।

जुष्टं यदा पश्यत्यन्यमीशमस्य महिमानमिति वीतशोकः ॥ ३.१.२

यदा पश्यः पश्यते रुक्मवर्णं कर्तारमीशं पुरुषं ब्रह्मयोनिम् ।

तदा विद्वान् पुण्यपापे विधूय निरञ्जनः परमं साम्यमुपैति ॥ ३.१.३

प्राणो ह्येष यः सर्वभूतैर्विभाति विजानन् विद्वान् भवते नातिवादी ।

आत्मक्रीड आत्मरतिः क्रियावानेष ब्रह्मविदां वरिष्ठः ॥ ३.१.४

सत्येन लभ्यस्तपसा ह्येष आत्मा सम्यग्ज्ञानेन ब्रह्मचर्येण नित्यम् ।

अन्तःशरीरे ज्योतिर्मयो हि शुभ्रो यं पश्यन्ति यतयः क्षीणदोषाः ॥ ३.१.५

सत्यमेव जयति नानृतं सत्येन पन्था विततो देवयानः ।

येनाक्रमन्त्य् ऋषयो ह्याप्तकामा यत्र तत् सत्यस्य परमं निधानम् ॥ ३.१.६

बृहच्च तद् दिव्यमचिन्त्यरूपं सूक्ष्माच्च तत् सूक्ष्मतरं विभाति ।

दूरात् सुदूरे तदिहान्तिके च पश्यत्स्विहैव निहितं गुहायाम् ॥ ३.१.७

न चक्षुषा गृह्यते नापि वाचा नान्यैर्देवैस्तपसा कर्मणा वा ।

ज्ञानप्रसादेन विशुद्धसत्त्वस्ततस्तु तं पश्यते निष्कलं ध्यायमानः ॥ ३.१.८

एषोऽणुरात्मा चेतसा वेदितव्यो यस्मिन् प्राणः पञ्चधा संविवेश ।

प्राणैश्चित्तं सर्वमोतं प्रजानां यस्मिन् विशुद्धे विभवत्येष आत्मा ॥ ३.१.९

यं यं लोकं मनसा संविभाति विशुद्धसत्त्वः कामयते यांश्च कामान् ।

तं तं लोकं जयते तांश्च कामांस्तस्मादात्मज्ञं ह्यर्चयेद् भूतिकामः ॥ ३.१.१०

तृतीयमुण्डकं द्वितीयः खण्डः

स वेदैतत् परमं ब्रह्म धाम यत्र विश्वं निहितं भाति शुभ्रम् ।

उपासते पुरुषं ये ह्यकामास्ते शुक्रमेतदतिवर्तन्ति धीराः ॥ ३.२.१

कामान् यः कामयते मन्यमानः स कामभिर्जायते तत्र तत्र ।

पर्याप्तकामस्य कृतात्मनस्तु इहैव सर्वे प्रविलीयन्ति कामाः ॥ ३.२.२

नायमात्मा प्रवचनेन लभ्यो न मेधया न बहुना श्रुतेन ।

यमेवैष वृणुते तेन लभ्यस्तस्यैष आत्मा विवृणुते तनुं स्वाम् ॥ ३.२.३

नायमात्मा बलहीनेन लभ्यो न च प्रमादात् तपसो वाप्यलिङ्गात् ।

एतैरुपायैर्यतते यस्तु विद्वांस्तस्यैष आत्मा विशते ब्रह्मधाम ॥ ३.२.४

सम्प्राप्यैनम् ऋषयो ज्ञानतृप्ताः कृतात्मानो वीतरागाः प्रशान्ताः ।

ते सर्वगं सर्वतः प्राप्य धीरा युक्तात्मानः सर्वमेवाविशन्ति ॥ ३.२.५

वेदान्तविज्ञानसुनिश्चितार्थाः संन्यासयोगाद् यतयः शुद्धसत्त्वाः ।

ते ब्रह्मलोकेषु परान्तकाले परामृताः परिमुच्यन्ति सर्वे ॥ ३.२.६

गताः कलाः पञ्चदश प्रतिष्ठा देवाश्च सर्वे प्रतिदेवतासु ।

कर्माणि विज्ञानमयश्च आत्मा परेऽव्यये सर्व एकीभवन्ति ॥ ३.२.७

यथा नद्यः स्यन्दमानाः समुद्रेऽस्तं गच्छन्ति नामरूपे विहाय ।

तथा विद्वान् नामरूपाद् विमुक्तः परात्परं पुरुषमुपैति दिव्यम् ॥ ३.२.८

स यो ह वै तत् परमं ब्रह्म वेद ब्रह्मैव भवति नास्याब्रह्मवित् कुले भवति ।

तरति शोकं तरति पाप्मानं गुहाग्रन्थिभ्यो विमुक्तोऽमृतो भवति ॥ ३.२.९

तदेतद् ऋचाभ्युक्तम् । क्रियावन्तः श्रोत्रिया ब्रह्मनिष्ठाः स्वयं जुह्वत एकर्षिं

श्रद्दयन्तः । तेषामेवैतां ब्रह्मविद्यां वदेत शिरोव्रतं विधिवद् यैस्तु चीर्णम् ॥ ३.२.१०

तदेतत् सत्यम् ऋषिरङ्गिराः पुरोवाच नैतदचीर्णव्रतोऽधीते ।

नमः परमऋषिभ्यो नमः परमऋषिभ्यः ॥ ३.२.११ ॥ समाप्तम् इदं मुण्डकम् ॥

ॐ भद्रं कर्णेभिः शृणुयाम देवाः । भद्रं पश्येम आक्षभिर्यजत्राः । स्थिरैरङ्गैस्
तुष्टुवाꣳ सस्तनूभिः । व्यशेम देवहितं यदायुः । स्वस्ति न इन्द्रो वृद्धश्रवाः ।
स्वस्ति नः पूषा विश्ववेदाः । स्वस्ति नस्ताक्ष्यो अरिष्टनेमिः । स्वस्ति नो
बृहस्पतिर्दधातु ॥ ॐ शान्तिः शान्तिः शान्तिः ॥

Sanskrit Grammar

Sandhis separated word by word पदच्छेद (प॰),
Verses in prose order अन्वय (अ॰),and with विभक्ति
Cases.

<u>Abbreviations</u>
Nouns

       m masculine, **f** feminine, **n** neuter; **V** vocative
       1/1 = vibhakti case from 1 to 7/number 1 to 3

Indeclinables (noninflected nouns or verbs) **0**
In Sanskrit the **adverbs** are mostly noninflected.

Verbs

       iii/1 = person i to iii / number 1 to 3
       PPP = Past Participle Passive = क्त
       PPA = Past Participle Active = क्तवत्
       PrPA = PresentParticiple Active = शतृ/ शानच्
       PoPP = PotentialParticiple Passive = य, तव्य,
       अनीयर् (gerund)
       तुमुन् = infinitive, in the sense of "to do"

Anusvara and Makara have been kept as they are in
Padacheda, to avoid over work. E.g. इदं should be
written as इदम् in Padacheda.

Sanskrit Literature frequently omits the verb – "is".
The words भवति, अस्ति etc. are implicit. E.g. verse
2.2.5 अमृतस्य एषः सेतुः (भवति) ॥

Since Sanskrit is an inflectional language, the **spelling of the same word** changes as per context or usage. Hence words can be **placed anywhere** in a sentence, as in poetic use, without change in meaning. The matrix shows how.

Verb inflections in Sanskrit – a sample chart

982 गम् गतौ – to go, also in the sense of attainment			
Present Tense Active voice लट् कर्त्तरि प्रयोग:			
Person/no	singular	dual	plural
Third	गच्छति[iii/1]	गच्छत:[iii/2]	गच्छन्ति[iii/3]
Second	गच्छसि[ii/1]	गच्छथ:[ii/2]	गच्छथ [ii/3]
First	गच्छामि[i/1]	गच्छाव: [i/2]	गच्छाम:[i/3]

Noun declensions in Sanskrit – a sample chart

Masculine stem, vowel अ ending			
(रू–आ–म्–अ) राम[m] Lord's name			
	singular[1]	dual [2]	plural [3]
1 Doer	राम:[1/1]	रामौ[1/2]	रामा:[1/3]
2 Object	रामम्[2/1]	रामौ[2/2]	रामान्[2/3]
3 by	रामेण[3/1]	रामाभ्याम्[3/2]	रामै:[3/3]
4 for	रामाय[4/1]	रामाभ्याम्[4/2]	रामेभ्य:[4/3]
5 from	रामात्[5/1]	रामाभ्याम्[5/2]	रामेभ्य:[5/3]
6 of	रामस्य[6/1]	रामयो:[6/2]	रामाणाम्[6/3]
7 in	रामे[7/1]	रामयो:[7/2]	रामेषु[7/3]
Vocative	हे राम[V/1]	हे रामौ[V/2]	हे रामा:[V/3]

Masculine stem, consonant त् ending		
मरुत्[m] Wind, Breeze, Air		

	singular[1]	dual[2]	plural[3]
1 Doer	मरुत् [1/1]	मरुतौ [1/2]	मरुतः [1/3]
2 Object	मरुतम् [2/1]	मरुतौ [2/2]	मरुतः [2/3]
3 by	मरुता [3/1]	मरुद्भ्याम् [3/2]	मरुद्भिः [3/3]
4 for	मरुते [4/1]	मरुद्भ्याम् [4/2]	मरुद्भ्यः [4/3]
5 from	मरुतः [5/1]	मरुद्भ्याम् [5/2]	मरुद्भ्यः [5/3]
6 of	मरुतः [6/1]	मरुतोः [6/2]	मरुताम् [6/3]
7 in	मरुति [7/1]	मरुतोः [7/2]	मरुत्सु [7/3]
Vocative	हे मरुत् [V/1]	हे मरुतौ [V/2]	हे मरुतः [V/3]

Moods and Tenses in Sanskrit

1	लट्	Present Tense
2	लङ्	Imperfect Past Tense – *now and back*
3	लिट्	Perfect Past Tense – *yesterday and back*
4	लुङ्	Aorist Past Tense – *distant past*
5	लुट्	First Future Tense – *tomorrow onwards*
6	लृट्	Second Future Tense – *now onwards*
7	लोट्	Imperative Mood – *request*
8	वि॰लिं॰	Potential Mood – *order* विधिलिङ्
9	आ॰लिं॰	Benedictive Mood – *blessing* आशीर्लिङ्
10	लृङ्	Conditional Mood – *if/then*

Conjugation process of Verb

वदन्ति = they say, they describe.

1st conjugation Root, Parasmaipadi.

1009 √ वदँ व्यक्तायां वाचि । to tell, relate, describe.

1.3.1 भूवादयो धातवः । वदँ = वद्‍अँ ।

1.3.2 उपदेशेऽजननुनासिक इत् । 1.3.9 तस्य लोपः । वद् ।

3.4.69 लः कर्मणि च भावे चाकर्मकेभ्यः । वद् ।

3.2.123 वर्तमाने लट् । 3.4.77 लस्य । वद् + लँट् ।

1.3.3 हलन्त्यम् । 1.3.9 तस्य लोपः । वद्+लँ ।

1.3.2 उपदेशेऽजननुनासिक इत् । 1.3.9तस्य लोपः । वद्+ल ।

3.4.78 तिप्तस्झिसिप्थस्थमिब्वस्मस् तातांझथासाथांध्वमिड्वहिमहिङ् ।

1.4.199 लः परस्मैपदम् । choose Parasmaipada affix.

वद्+झि । we are conjugating third person

1.4.101 तिङस्त्रीणि त्रीणि प्रथममध्यमोत्तमाः ।

1.4.102 तान्येकवचनद्विवचनबहुवचनान्येकशः । वद्+झि । plural

1.4.108 शेषे प्रथमः । वद्+झि । this is called "प्रथमः" i.e. the **first and most** used in language, third person.

3.4.113 तिङ्‌शित्सार्वधातुकम् । वद्+झि ।

3.1.68 कर्त्तरि शप् । वद्+शप्+झि ।

3.4.113तिङ्‌शित्सार्वधातुकम् । वद्+शप्+झि ।

7.1.3 झोऽन्तः । वद्+शप्+ अन्ति ।

1.3.3 हलन्त्यम्। 1.3.8लशक्वतद्धिते । 1.3.9तस्य लोपः ।वद्+अ+अन्ति ।

6.1.97 अतो गुणे । वद्+अन्ति । sandhi drops the अकारः ।

8.3.24 नश्चापदान्तस्य झलि । वद् + अंति । Anusvara appears

8.4.58 अनुस्वारस्य ययि परसवर्णः । वद् + अन्ति ।

Anusvara again changes to नकारः ।

वद् + अन्ति = वदन्ति [iii/3 लट्] । iii = 3rd person, 3 = plural.
Third person plural, Present Tense.

Declension process of Noun

ब्रह्म = Brahma. The Lord. Highest Intelligence.
Stem Brahman ब्रह्मन् n $\longrightarrow$ ब्रह्म neuter Nominative $1/1$
The Great Lord. The Invisible presence.
1.2.45 अर्थवदधातुरप्रत्ययः प्रातिपदिकम् । ब्रह्मन्
1.2.46 कृत्तद्धितसमासाश्च । 3.1.1 प्रत्ययः । 3.1.2 परश्च ।
4.1.1 ङ्याप्प्रातिपदिकात् । 4.1.2 स्वौजस-
मौट्छष्टाभ्याम्भिस्ङेभ्याम्भ्यस्ङसिभ्याम्भ्यस्ङसोसाम्ङ्योस्सुप् ।
1.4.104 विभक्तिश्च । 1.4.103 सुपः = use one of these
vibhakti suffix. ब्रह्मन् + सुँ ।
1.4.22 ब्येकयोर्द्विवचनैकवचने = singular number taken.
ब्रह्मन् + सुँ ।
7.1.23 स्वमोर्नपुंसकात् । 2.4.13 यस्मात्प्रत्ययविधिस्तदादि
प्रत्ययेऽङ्गम् । 6.4.1 अङ्गस्य । 1st and 2nd case Vibhakti
drops for neuter stem. ब्रह्मन् ।
1.4.17 स्वादिष्वसर्वनामस्थाने । The word gets पदसंज्ञा ।
ब्रह्मन् ।
8.2.7 न लोपः प्रातिपदिकान्तस्य । Final नकार drops.
ब्रह्म $n1/1$ ।

Neuter. First case nominative singular. **Brahma.**
The Highest. The Supreme. Shiva. Purusha. Tao.
The Beautiful, The Love, The Infinite, The Divine.
Any name is **Him.**
All directions point to **It.** Every form is **She.**

References

https://www.ashtangayoga.info/philosophy/sanskrit-and-devanagari/transliteration-tool/
http://spokensanskrit.org/
http://bhagavadgita.org.in/sanskrit
https://upanishads.org.in/
https://www.sanskritworld.in/index/Sanskrittool
http://ashtadhyayi.com/dhatu/
http://tdil-dc.in/san/skt_gen/generators.html#
Audio Chant
https://www.youtube.com/playlist?list=PLzz9KpK4CcMMRNzBr95tQeuOEl9RJW8Ao
https://www.youtube.com/watch?v=bT8hC6MkGH8

Sitarama Sastri – The Upanishads – Isa, Kena & Mundaka Vol 1 – 1st – 1905 - V. C. Seshacharri, Madras.

Swami Sharvananda – Mundaka and Mandukya Upanishads – 1st – 1920 - Sri Ramakrishna Math, Madras.

KLV Sastry & Anantarama Sastri – Sabda Manjari 1961– Reprint - 2013 – RS Vadhyar & Sons, Palghat.

Gita Press – मुण्डकोपनिषद् सानुवाद शांकरभाष्यसहित – 26th Reprint - 2013 – Gita Press, Gorakhpur.

Swami Devarupananda – मन्त्रपुष्पम् - 4th – 2010 – Ramakrishna Math, Khar, Mumbai.

Sri Sri Ravi Shankar - Upanishad Vol1 - Ishavasya Kena Katha Yogasara - 1st – 2017 – Sri Sri Publications Trust, Bangalore

Ashwini Kumar Aggarwal – Dhatupatha of Panini – 2nd – 2017 – Devotees of Sri Sri Ravi Shankar Ashram, Punjab.

Epilogue

It is worthwhile to soak in the Master's words. For a long time it may seem unnecessary to seek help and guidance, but when a Master arrives in life, it is best to listen carefully and implement earnestly.

Fortunate are those who are compelled to turn to a higher power, who go seeking for that which is beyond the senses, who have had enough of this world and its ways.

सर्वे भवन्तु सुखिनः । सर्वे सन्तु निरामयाः ।

सर्वे भद्राणि पश्यन्तु । मा कश्चिद् दुःख भाग्भवेत् ॥

ॐ शान्तिः शान्तिः शान्तिः ॥

When faith has blossomed in life,
Every step is led by the Divine.

Sri Sri Ravi Shankar

Om Namah Shivaya

जय गुरुदेव

www.ingramcontent.com/pod-product-compliance
Lightning Source LLC
LaVergne TN
LVHW040136180726
843489LV00005B/1790